A Denomination Looks at Itself

A Denomination Looks at Itself

ANTHONY CAMPOLO, JR.

Judson Press, Valley Forge

A DENOMINATION LOOKS AT ITSELF

To the Most Significant
People in My Life — Peggy, Lisa, and Bart

Editorial Note

Anthony Campolo, Jr., has been invited by Judson Press (which is associated with the American Baptist Board of Education and Publication) to write this book because of his unique qualifications as a professional sociologist and a former American Baptist pastor. He has been given complete freedom to make his own interpretations on the basis of his analysis of the sociological aspects of the Roper study of the American Baptist Convention.

In publishing this book, therefore, no censorship of any kind has been applied to Dr. Campolo's work and, conversely, no denominational endorsement of any kind is implied. The views expressed are strictly those of the author and do not necessarily reflect those of the American Baptist Convention, the American Baptist Board of Education and Publication, or Judson Press.

Preface

THE SOCIOLOGY OF RELIGION is a disenchanting subject. It requires that the religious institutions and practices of society
be viewed in as scientific a manner as possible. Such a procedure, however, often has a devastating effect on many of
the things which people consider sacred, for many aspects
of religious life which were previously deemed as God-
ordained come to be viewed by the sociologist as being
culturally determined. Beliefs and commitments are thus
oftentimes recognized to be controlled by socioeconomic forces.
Such an understanding of religious behavior can create serious doubts and questions about one's own particular religious orientation. Many of the features which one has considered to be based on divine revelation and to be eternally
sacred come to be viewed as timebound societal creations.
Within such an academic discipline a person may easily lose
his religious convictions.

Some may ask whether such a discipline is recommended
for Christians. My answer is a resounding "Yes!" I think that
it is essential for the Christian to understand which aspects
of his faith are cultural representations and which transcend

the culture and have eternal moorings. With such discernment he will be able to free himself from the idolatrous tendency to worship the products of his culture as though they were God-ordained. The sociology of religion prepares an individual to recognize with greater clarity those things which are eternal and worthy of maintaining with reverence.

Because this particular book is written from the perspective of the sociology of religion, it therefore possesses certain "demythologizing" traits. The book focuses upon one denomination, the American Baptist Convention, seeking to understand something of its program and policy from a scientific point of view. Objectivity can seem offensive to those who are subjectively involved, however, and there is much in this volume which will stir negative reactions from those who are endeavoring to serve Christ within the context of this denomination. My only claim is that I have tried to maintain impartiality, which may mean that I have included something to offend everyone.

I do not want to suggest that this book maintains pure objectivity, even if that were possible in the social sciences. My personal theoretical perspective of society may have a distorting effect on the presentation, particularly in reference to the importance I place on the influence of social class on religious behavior, in that I believe economic factors to be very significant in this area. Also, my conservative theological beliefs will be evident in places.

The denominational officials who requested me to write this book should be commended for turning to those outside of their organization to study the nature of the denomination. The Roper Research Associates, whose statistical material is used in this volume, are a professional polling organization operating out of New York City. Even so, those who are responsible for the publications of the denominational publishing house might easily have called upon some executive within the American Baptist structure to write this kind of book. Though the personal involvement of such an executive would have hindered the objectivity of the presentation, he probably would have written a book that cast his organization in a more favorable light. The executives who turned to outsiders for this type of study possessed an admirable desire to learn the truth about themselves even if the truth was not flattering. Though an American Baptist, I have never been part of the executive staff of the denomination although I have held elected offices.

I want to thank Dr. Norman H. Maring, whose example made me want to be a teacher, and Dr. Paul M. van Buren, who showed me how to understand religion from a secular perspective. Most of all I want to express gratitude to my wife, Peggy, whose patience, suggestions, and typing made this book possible.

ANTHONY CAMPOLO, JR.

Contents

1

Introduction

MANY PEOPLE CLAIM THAT denominational leaders are insensitive to the thinking and wishes of the rank-and-file church members. This is the most common accusation leveled at major Protestant denominations by those who have become disenchanted with them. Critics assume that there is a high level of alienation between those who formulate denominational policies and the members of the local churches among whom these policies are propagated. Denominational leaders are said to be "out of touch with the man in the pew," unaware of his theological and social sensitivities. Consequently, it is contended, these leaders formulate programs, take stands on social issues, maintain theological perspectives, and possess orientations to society which are out of harmony with those represented by Protestantism's "silent majority."

Such factors are often cited to explain the declining financial support which most denominations have experienced over the past few years. Critics contend that the people in the churches can hardly be expected to underwrite programs that are often in diametrical opposition to their own views. They say that unless the leaders perceive the dispositions of their constituencies and construct policies to harmonize with them, there will be an increasing tendency for members to withhold contributions from denominational coffers and for churches to steer courses of independency.

These warnings have been strongly expressed in reference to the support which most major denominations have given to the Interreligious Foundation for Community Organization (IFCO). Since there appears to be some connection between IFCO and certain black militants, the ire of many usually docile supporters of Protestant denominations has been raised. Many have suggested that if denominations are to survive, they had best not alienate some of their most loyal bill-payers.

These general conditions are particularly true of the American Baptist Convention. The leaders of this denomination have grounds for their extreme sensitivity to criticism. They experienced two major schisms during the Fundamentalist Controversy, along with the withdrawal of hundreds of churches that became discontented with the organization's "liberal" orientation. The church polity maintained by American Baptists allows any offended congregation to withdraw from denominational affiliation simply by vote of its members. Such events and conditions have made American Baptist leaders especially vulnerable to the threats of further losses by those who question their policies.

Any denominational innovation or departure from traditional ideas must be carefully introduced, lest a resulting reaction prove too costly. Consequently, American Baptist leaders have endeavored to utilize every available means to understand the disposition of the church membership and thus accurately to predict the reactions which denominational programs will elicit.

One means which was recently employed was to call upon an independent polling agency to analyze the nature of the denomination's constituency and to evaluate its opinions on a variety of significant issues. With the use of sociological tools of research this agency endeavored to evaluate how the members regarded their denominational program, what was considered to be the role of the church in modern society, and what American Baptists believed in respect to certain pertinent theological issues. The report was presented to the General Council and the boards of the related agencies in October, 1969.

The book you hold in your hands contains a presentation of the results of that study and an interpretation of what those results suggest for the program planning of the denomination. It also provides an illustration of how sociological techniques can be employed to increase the rapport between denominational leaders and church members. Therefore, it is a case study which should be of significance for persons concerned with the problem of communication between those in executive ecclesiastical positions and the people in the local congregations, not only in the American Baptist Convention, but in other denominations as well.

The Roper Study

In 1968 the American Baptist Convention employed Roper Research Associates, Inc., of New York, to conduct a survey of its constituent members. The expressed purpose of the study was to assess the effectiveness of the denomination's communication media. The Roper survey was one part of a larger study which examined the whole area of denominational communications.

Prior to this survey the leaders of the American Baptist Convention had continually endeavored to inform local church members of the many activities carried on by their denominational organizations. They wanted their constituency to know of the accomplishments of the ABC and its related agencies in home and foreign missionary work, Christian higher education, publishing, Christian social action projects, evangelism, and similar areas. To this end they had used magazines, pamphlets, special speakers, films, and radio and television programs. Seeking to evaluate how well they had accomplished their purpose, therefore, they employed Roper Research Associates to help them study the level of their effectiveness and to develop means for improvement.

In addition to this primary purpose, the survey was also

to have the following aims, which for the general reader are far more significant (Roper, page 1):*

(1) To explore which issues and interests of the American Baptist Convention are foremost among church members today and where church members stand on them.

(2) To investigate knowledge of and attitudes towards the American Baptist Convention by church members.

(3) To determine the extent of knowledge and the image church members have of the leadership at Valley Forge in terms of both awareness and attitudes.

How the Study Was Conducted

The Roper organization gathered information for this study by interviewing a nationwide cross section of the adult members of the denomination. It sought to gain data from 1,000 persons who would be representative of the denomination as a whole.

Becoming curious as to whether or not this sample was sufficiently large to give a valid evaluation of an organization with almost one and one-half million members, I sought the advice and opinion of statisticians who are expert in such questions. They informed me that a sample of this size was probably ample for the purposes stated. If the study had dealt with only one factor or question, a person could have calculated the precision and confidence level which the sample provided. However, this study dealt with more than eighty questions, so that such a simple procedure would be impossible. Rather, a person would have to figure separately the mean deviation of each of the factors studied and then estimate how large a sample would have been necessary to keep the mean deviation at the desired level.

Instead, the Roper Associates simply took what they considered to be an adequate number to insure representation of all segments of the total population. A careful review of their sampling will show that every type of member (re-

---

*All references to *A Study of Communications of the American Baptist Convention* (New York: Roper Research Associates, 1969) will be designated by the parenthetical notation (Roper, page ——).

gardless of the size church in which he holds membership or the location of that church) was given proper representation. What is particularly significant is that each of the respondents was personally interviewed, insuring almost a 100 percent response to the questionnaire. The Roper Associates described the survey procedure as follows (Roper, pages 2 and 3):

All associations (excluding those in Puerto Rico, Oklahoma and Brackett-Morrell) were grouped into the nine geographic regions and listed in descending order of *resident* church membership within each region. Fifty associations were selected at random proportionate to church membership. Within each of the 50 associations, three churches were selected — again at random proportionate to resident church membership.

The names of the 150 churches selected were sent to the national office of the American Baptist Convention. The national office wrote to the ministers of each of the churches selected, informing them that a survey was planned and asking for a *complete* list of resident members (indicating, however, which were under 18 years of age).

In cases where individual churches declined to participate in the study, substitutions were made within the same association and to match the original church as closely as possible as to size and location.

The complete church member lists were turned over to the Roper organization. Since it was planned to interview 20 people per association, six or seven names were selected from each church (two 7's, one 6), again at random proportionate to resident church membership. A substitute list was also drawn at random from each church list, so that substitutions could be made for those drawn in the original list who refused the interview, or for other reasons were not available for an interview.

Since respondents were selected on a completely random basis proportionate to membership, the distribution of interviews between men and women could be assumed to represent enrollment by sex as it exists in the total membership of the American Baptist Convention. To insure that substitutions had not distorted the male-female ratio in any way, a tabulation by sex of members drawn in the original sample was made, and compared with a tabulation by sex of those interviewed. Respondents in the study closely matched the male-female ratio in the original draw.

After the names were selected from church lists, a letter was mailed by the Roper organization to each prospective respondent explaining that the study was being conducted and asking for cooperation when the Roper interviewer called for an appointment. A separate letter from the National Office of the American Baptist Convention addressed simply to church members was enclosed which further explained the study. Copies of these letters are included in the report. At no time was the name of any respondent — or prospective respondent — revealed by the Roper organization to the National Office.

All interviews were carried out in person by Roper interviewers in the homes of respondents. A total of 997 interviews was completed. The bulk of the interviewing was conducted in two periods — from November 21, 1968 to December 21, 1968 and from January 13, 1969 to February 1, 1969. A few interviews were carried out between the two main interviewing periods, and a few were carried out between February 1 and February 15. Interviewing time was necessarily sporadic because lists of members from the churches came in irregularly over a considerable period of time.

The questions themselves were drawn up by Roper Research Associates, who are experts in the intricate process of posing questions in an "unloaded" form. However, members of the denomination's executive staff assisted them by specifying which areas of the American Baptist life should be examined. The fact that certain areas were chosen for study while other areas were ignored represents a kind of bias and represents a possible weakness in the study. The best research methodology does not provide for those being studied to determine which sectors of their activities are to be surveyed. In spite of such limiting weaknesses the study seems to have been fair, and the questionnaire was sufficiently well constructed to provide the basis for an objective approach to the evaluation of the denomination.

The Roper study provides a good description of the attitudes and opinions represented in the American Baptist Convention. However, a description is not an explanation. Empirical data need to be interpreted within a theoretical context which will give it meaning. Though the Roper study provides some information as to *what* attitudes, beliefs, and dispositions exist within this denomination, it does not endeavor to explain *why* they exist or what their significance might be.

In this book the findings of the Roper study are interpreted within the context of theories which are prevalent in the field of the sociology of religion. While these explanations may, on the one hand, bias the statistics to support claims they were not intended to support, they may, on the other hand, give the facts significant meanings which are of great relevance to those who are trying to understand this denomination. This approach may possibly distort the description which the Roper organization has so carefully constructed. Yet, if sociology is to go beyond mere description, such risks must be taken.

2

American Baptists—Sect or Church?

THE FINDINGS OF THE ROPER STUDY will be used first of all to locate American Baptists in relation to American society as a whole. Their social location, or social class standing, has a great deal of significance for the style of their church life.

American Baptists Are Upper Middle Class

The Roper study indicates that most American Baptists are in the upper half of society in respect to socioeconomic factors. This conclusion is derived from a survey of the occupations of the heads of the households represented in the sample.

Some may argue that there are many other factors influencing class standing (i.e., place of residence, family connections, income, education, political ties, etc.) and that a conclusion based solely upon the occupations of heads of households is not justified. However, although the experts on social stratification, such as W. Lloyd Warner,[1] outline the significance of various factors which determine class standing, they generally conclude that the occupation of the head of the household is probably the most significant. Occupation exercises a control on the other factors and to a great degree determines income, residence, life style, and political tendencies. Since the Roper Research Associates were not making a stratification study primarily, and were interested in class standing only coincidentally, their choice of occupation as the basic index for socioeconomic evaluation was probably sound.

Each interviewee was asked to pick from the following list the occupation of the head of his household (Item 82 in the Roper questionnaire which is bound with *A Study of Communications*).

Top management, top talent, and major professional
Executive, administrative, lesser professional
Owner — small retail store or business
Technicians, minor administrative and low supervisory
White collar, clerical (non-supervisory)
Skilled and semi-skilled labor
Unskilled labor
Service and protective workers
Salesmen
Farmers (owners and managers)
Military personnel
Housewife
Retired
Other

These occupations were graded in terms of class standings. The results were then compared with the distribution of the population of the nation with respect to class standings. The resulting figures indicate that American Baptists are somewhat upscale in socioeconomic level to a degree that is significantly greater than the sample of the population of the entire nation (Roper, page 75):

	American Baptists	Recent study
	%	%
Upper (A, A-, B+)	10	6
Upper middle (B, B-)	22	18
Middle (C+, C)	46	45
Lower (C-, D+, D)	18	31
No answer	2	–

A survey of the educational level provided further justification for the above conclusion, for it revealed that American Baptists evidenced a higher level of education than the general population (Roper, page 75):

	American Baptists	Recent study
	%	%
Grade school or less	15	21
High school	53	55
College	32	22
No answer	*	1

*Less than 0.5 percent

The realization that American Baptist church members tend to be upper middle class in socioeconomic standing may come as a surprise to many students of social stratification. Past studies have suggested, and scholars have assumed, that Baptists were to be identified with lower-class social groupings. For example, Herbert Schneider published the following table in 1952:[2]

SOCIAL CLASS PROFILES OF AMERICAN RELIGIOUS GROUPS

	Upper	Middle	Lower	N
Christian Scientist	24.8%	36.5%	38.7%	(137)
Episcopal	24.1	33.7	42.2	(590)
Congregational	23.9	42.6	33.5	(376)
Presbyterian	21.9	40.0	38.1	(961)
Jewish	21.8	32.0	46.2	(537)
Reformed	19.1	31.3	49.6	(131)
Methodist	12.7	35.6	51.7	(2,100)
Lutheran	10.9	36.1	53.0	(723)
Christian	10.0	35.4	54.6	(370)
Protestant (smaller bodies)	10.0	27.3	62.7	(888)
Roman Catholic	8.7	24.7	66.6	(2,390)
Baptist	8.0	24.0	68.0	(1,381)
Mormon	5.1	28.6	66.3	(175)
No preference	13.3	26.0	60.7	(466)
Protestant (undesignated)	12.4	24.1	63.5	(460)
Atheist, Agnostic	33.3	46.7	20.0	(15)
No Answer or "Don't Know"	11.0	29.5	59.5	(319)

The Roper study provides evidence that American Baptists are exceptional in their social standing and are atypical of the status generally attributed to Baptists. With respect to class standings it seems clear that they are above other Baptist groups.

This upper-middle-class standing of American Baptists represents a rise above their earlier status. In the nineteenth century this denomination drew its members from a lower socioeconomic group. However, the zealous kind of religious life practiced by these earlier Baptists tended to create a dedication to work and thrift which resulted in an improved social position. John Wesley (whose Methodist religious movement possessed many of the same characteristics inherent in the Baptist tradition) perceptively explained this phenomenon:

> . . . religion must necessarily produce both industry and frugality, and these cannot but produce riches. . . . We ought not to prevent people from being diligent and frugal; we *must* exhort all Christians to gain all they can, and to save all they can; that is, in effect, to grow rich.[3]

In sociological terminology, the strict adherence by Baptists and Methodists to "the Protestant ethic" was responsible for this upward mobility.[4]

The Significance of the Class Factor

Sociologists since Ernst Troeltsch have been aware that class standing exercises many significant influences upon the life style of churches. Troeltsch was the first to set up the classic typology which distinguished the kind of religiosity expressed by the upper classes, which he labeled "ecclesiastical," as distinguished from the "sectarian" religion of the lower classes. For our purposes these two types of religion can be characterized by the following contrasts:

Sect	Ecclesia
1. Membership by conversion (i.e., a mystical experience). Only adult believers are admitted.	1. Membership through birth (i.e., children are nurtured into membership through an educational process).

2. Worship services are highly informal and charged with emotion.	2. Worship services are formal and rationally ordered.
3. There is no hierarchy of leadership. Leaders gain their authority through charismatic gifts.	3. There is a well-defined hierarchy of leadership. Leaders gain their authority by a rational means (i.e., seminary education).
4. Members believe that they alone are the heirs of God's salvation.	4. Members do not claim any exclusive religious position for themselves. They do not view membership in their group as a prerequisite to salvation.
5. Members tend to regard the general culture as doomed. They ask their converts to be disengaged from "worldly" activities and to be primarily involved in "religious" (i.e., church) activities.	5. Members tend to accept the culture as good. They are highly involved in the societal institutions and regard the church as but one part of their lives.

Sociologists generally assume that as people move from lower class to upper middle class they will shed the characteristics of sectarian religion and assume those of an ecclesiastical syndrome. If this assumption is valid, a shift in the class standing of American Baptists must have been accompanied by corresponding changes in their style of church life. Therefore, let us try to identify some specific instances of how this class shift has affected the denomination.

First, in referring to the chart of contrasts between a sect and an ecclesia, we observe that a shift to the upper middle class would be correlated with a de-emphasis on the revivalistic type of Christianity which won new members through traumatic conversions, and such a shift would evidence a growing tendency toward leading children and youth into a Christian experience through education and nurture. Indeed, the Roper study can offer some substantiation that this shift is taking place. When asked to choose from a list of seven items those issues and activities which should be the major concerns of the American Baptist Convention, members gave Christian education the most support by far. On the other hand, evangelism (traditionally related to winning converts) ran a poor third in the standings and failed to gain any support from the majority of the respondents (Roper, page 62):

Number of respondents	997
Christian education	72%
Home missions	59
Evangelism	48
Foreign missions	43
Civil rights and race relations	43
Schools and colleges	42
Theological education	35
Don't know	1

The declining emphasis on conversion is further revealed in another part of the Roper study which shows that only 3 percent of those now in American Baptist churches came into membership through such a religious experience (Roper, page 77). This finding is vastly different from the situation in the nineteenth century when, in accord with a sectarian-type religious style, this denomination made great gains through winning converts.[5]

These findings seem to fit sociological expectations as they indicate that, in keeping with the changes in class status, American Baptists seem less inclined toward traditional evangelism and more supportive of programs of Christian nurture. The above observation should not be construed as a value judgment on traditional evangelism but simply as an explanation of its declining popularity within an increasingly middle-class denomination.

Second, it should be noted that a shift to the middle-class church style (the ecclesia) would be marked by a decline in emotionalism within church worship services. Also, a rationalistically prescribed service with an increasingly high level of formality would be more and more in vogue.

Although the Roper study offers no empirical data to support this claim, it is clearly evident that formality and rationality have increasingly marked the Sunday services of American Baptists. More and more their churches use the robed choir, the robed minister, the lighted candles, the divided chancel, and the observances of the liturgical year. The informality which marked this group's revivalistic religiosity during the late nineteenth century is quickly vanishing. The sermons are increasingly well-thought-out expositions on "relevant" issues rather than the spontaneous exhortations that marked that earlier era "when men preached from their hearts." Such amens as once punctuated the emotionally charged homilies of the Baptist preacher would probably shock the typically staid American Baptist congregation of today. If some nineteenth-century Baptist forefathers were resurrected to visit many of today's formal suburban American Baptist churches, they would not believe that they were in Baptist churches at all. They might think they were in Episcopal, or possibly Presbyterian, churches. We would have to explain to them the changes which have come with shifts in class standings.

Third, the type of leadership which congregations require for the middle-class ecclesia is notably different from that required by the lower-class sect. Whereas the sect expects that its pastor will be charismatically endowed along with evidence of a "divine calling," the middle-class church is concerned with the academic qualifications of the minister. To use the categorizations of Max Weber, the sectarian group tends to evidence an elective affinity to *charismatic* leadership while the ecclesia tends to require leadership which is chosen on a *rational* basis. Weber maintains that the rational type of leader which would be evident in the middle-class church would have the following characteristics: (1) That he gains his position through a testing process, (2) that he has formal training for his position, (3) that he regards his position as a full-time occupation, (4) that he considers himself as part of a leadership hierarchy which guarantees him upward mobility as a reward for seniority and objectively evaluated accomplishment.[6] Let us see how each of these Weberian expectations is gradually being met by the denomination.

Many state conventions have adopted conditions for ordination which would require candidates for the ministry to have completed both a college and a seminary education. The New Jersey Baptist Convention is a prime example of such a practice. The old days in which a man with a couple of years of training at a Bible institute and a vision from God could qualify for ordination seem destined to be permanently passing from the American Baptist scene.

One should add to the above an apparent tendency of the denomination to eliminate part-time pastors. State conventions, in many instances, are underwriting the salaries of pastors in small churches so that these pastors can be "full-time." Smaller churches are being urged to consolidate in order to provide a rational way for providing a proper ministry for their people. Thus, the American Baptist churches seem to be eliminating the lay ministers, with the possible exception of seminary students. This move seems somewhat strange in light of the fact that over half of the churches have less than a hundred members and would find the use of lay pastors extremely feasible. However, the tendency toward middle-class status in these small churches requires rational-type leaders on a full-time basis even when economic factors make such arrangements difficult.

Whereas local churches once controlled the ordination process, the authority has gradually passed into the domain of the associations. Ordination councils evaluate the credentials of the ministerial candidate and quiz him to ascertain his theological competence. More and more the ordination council becomes, in Weberian fashion, a testing of the potential pastor to determine his rational preparation for this role. Also, the seminaries are generally demanding that the candidate complete a Minnesota Multiphasic Personality Inventory. In this way persons with personality irregularities and defects can be spotted and discouraged from entering the pastorate. By these tests it is possible to ferret out and eliminate the kinds of persons who are overly individualistic, do not evidence capacities for working well in team efforts, possess psychological idiosyncrasies (i.e., hearing voices, seeing visions), or lack a well-rounded spectrum of interests.

One wonders how the apostle Paul would have made out in such a testing program. Certainly some tests would suggest that he had psychotic tendencies (as indicated by his experiences on the way to Damascus), had too many individualistic traits (as supported by the fact that he could not get along with his associate pastors, Mark and Barnabas), and possessed a tendency to take his work too seriously (he said, "for me to live is Christ"). These would be marks against him. The apostle Peter would not have made it as a rational type either.

Another evidence of the rationalizing tendency in the leadership of American Baptist churches is the movement away from congregational forms of church government to presbyterian types of polity. Of course this is to be expected when one considers that rational middle-class leadership shies away from the non-structured, non-hierarchical make-up of sectarian-type religious organization traditionally evident in Baptist churches. A rational ecclesiastical hierarchy in which the properly trained bureaucratic-type clergyman can find security and expect regular improvements in status and position is more fitting for the middle-class syndrome. In these respects, the presbyterian and episcopalian systems have the advantage.

Consider another characteristic of the shift away from sectarian styles. As the movement to middle-class status occurs, there should be a relinquishing of the exclusivistic attitudes toward salvation so evident in lower-class religion. An increasingly liberal disposition toward differing religious convictions should be demonstrated. Once again sociological expectations appear to be met.

There is an emerging theology of universal salvation evident in American Baptist circles. This is a belief that Jesus completed his work on the cross for all men; therefore, all men enjoy the benefits of his salvation whether they accept the teachings of Christianity or not. However, a careful review of this emerging position will reveal that it is not universalism in the traditional sense.[7]

What is being maintained is that God's salvation is meant for the whole universe (which includes social structures, institutions, economic systems, etc.) and is not just for those individuals who believe the gospel. It is a belief that God wills the redemption of the social systems which have emerged during the evolution of civilizations.

The claim is made that God wills those suprapersonal institutions, which regulate human behavior, to function in a righteous fashion. In maintaining that the salvation of God reaches beyond individual men to re-create social entities such as the state, the business complex, the educational systems and the recreational institutions, a worldwide (i.e., universal) dimension to God's activity in history is suggested. This is in accord with Romans 8:22 ff., which points out that all sectors of God's creation are to be saved through the redemptive work of Jesus.

Unfortunately, many who argue against the emerging universalism in American Baptist circles are not aware of this meaning and wrongly assume that what is being suggested *is* that everyone goes to heaven regardless of willingness to accept Jesus as personal savior. This new universalism does not focus on what will happen in the after life but, in typical middle-class fashion, is concerned with what will happen to *this* world.

That such a universalism is becoming a live theological option for American Baptists is evident by the constant references to it in debates and discussions in denominational meetings, pastors' conferences, and seminaries. The cause for this growing manifestation of universalism cannot simply be attributed to some encroaching liberal theology. It may be the result of the new mindset of those Baptists who, in moving up the socioeconomic ladder, have abandoned their sectarian exclusiveness for a doctrine of salvation which encompasses the whole world, typical of members of an ecclesia.

The declining sectarian exclusiveness of American Baptists is further evident in their beliefs about church membership. Although American Baptists never believed that they were the only Christians (except for a very small minority in the Landmark tradition),[8] they have usually maintained that believers' baptism by immersion is the legitimate form of baptism and the only ground for membership in their churches. This exclusiveness is fading.

The Roper study indicates that 53 percent of American Baptists now approve of "open membership" whereby a person who holds membership in another church but has never been baptized by immersion can be accepted as a member in a Baptist congregation. A significant minority of 42 percent still maintain the older traditional position of accepting as church members only those who have experienced immersion. However, this minority will probably diminish in size and significance, due to the fact that the younger members of the denomination tend toward the more liberal position. The survey reports that 62 percent of members between 18 and 35 years of age favor open membership as opposed to 53 percent in the 35-to-54 age bracket and only 48 percent of those 55 years and over who favor open membership. When the denomination eventually falls into the hands of those who now comprise the youngest group, then one may assume that the more liberal position will triumph. Baptists will come to treat this distinctive trait with less seriousness and assume the more open attitude toward other Christians. The old sectarian mentality thus seems doomed to a gradual death during the next few decades (Roper, page 53).

	Approve of transfer by letter	Accepted only if baptized by immersion
	%	%
Total church members	53	42
Age		
18-34	62	35
35-54	53	40
55 and over	48	46
Educational level		
College	66	29
High school	49	46
Grade school	40	52
Geographic area		
Northeast	66	29
Midwest	44	49
South	45	52
Far West	50	44
Race		
White	54	41
Non-white	45	46

The growing support for the ecumenical movement among
American Baptists also supports the claim that the denomination is moving away from its former sectarian exclusiveness.
In a larger sense the middle-class attitude of shunning sectarian differences may be ultimately responsible for creating
the conditions for a merger of the major American denominations. A merger might be expected of religious organizations
which had assumed the ecclesia typology.

Still another mark of the changing social status of American
Baptists is the emerging belief that social action programs
are legitimate religious concerns. Sectarian religionists tend
to retreat from involvements in programs of societal reconstruction. They believe that this world is doomed to a process
of moral and social decay which will be climaxed with the
cataclysmic return of Jesus. They are convinced that there
is nothing that can be done to stem this tide of history as it
flows to its inexorable end. Programs of social reform cannot
restrain the inevitable. Like bailing water from the hull of
the sinking *Titanic,* the results are not worth the effort. Society
is doomed and those who try to save it, regardless of how
admirable their concern and motivation, are wasting their
energies.

The sectarian religion requires its members to spend all
their energies in "saving souls" from the impending doom.
The followers are convinced that the world is in its "last days"
and that saving souls is the only venture that is reasonable
in light of this fact. Thus, in this view, Christian social
concern has value only insofar as it makes those who are
served more receptive to the gospel. The good deeds done
for suffering society may gain a hearing for the gospel. However, except as "bait" to catch the lost sinner, social action
can accomplish no ultimately significant results.

Perhaps the attitude of these often socially disinherited
Christians stems from their rejection of a society which they
feel has rejected them. Lower-class sectarians have often
been so badly treated by society that a pronouncement of
divine judgment on the world would be welcomed as justice.
Since this world offers them so little in the way of joy and
rewards, the attention of the socially disinherited becomes

fixed on the next world beyond the skies, where "he has put down the mighty from their thrones, and exalted those of low degree" (Luke 1:52). What does it matter if there is social injustice and suffering in this world if one believes that this world will shortly pass away and the "saved" will be transported to heaven where "tears shall be wiped away"? Why be concerned about improving a social system which has oppressed the people of God and is consequently decaying and moving toward final destruction? The socially disinherited can accept joyfully the fact that a world which has rejected them will be rejected by God. Why get involved in trying to improve such a world?

On the other hand, the middle-class Christians are not disposed to such wholesale judgment of the social order. After all, society has dealt favorably with them and therefore cannot be all that bad. A society which has afforded a good life must itself be good, although in need of improvement.

The middle-class church members can affirm this world and hope to improve it and make it an even more blessed place in which to live. Contrary to the world-denying tendencies of sectarians, they believe that the world is good and that history gives evidence that the kingdom of God is emerging in this world.[9] Since God loved the world, should not they do likewise? Do Christians not pray for the kingdom to come "on earth even as it is in heaven"? Is not the gospel the good news about the things God is doing to renew his world? Surely those who are involved in social reconstruction are laborers together with God in the salvation of the world. So goes much middle-class thinking.

From what is stated above it is evident that the lower-class sectarian will have an attitude toward the social action programs of the denomination very different from that of a member of a middle-class church. The argument over the emphasis on social involvement in the programming of the American Baptist Convention consequently will be influenced by the class factor.

Upon close examination, those who favor a total commitment of the denomination to traditional evangelism will tend to be of lower socioeconomic status. One might also discover that some of the opposition to the growing tendency of the denomination to become involved in contemporary social issues is actually a disguised resentment against the growing middle-class orientation of the American Baptist Convention held by that diminishing lower-class segment which remains in the constituency.

If the theoretical assumptions which have been made are to be verified, there must be some evidence that the transition to middle-class status for American Baptists is positively correlated with a growing interest in social concerns. The results of the Roper study are not disappointing in this respect, for they show that sociological expectations have been met.

In some of the most interesting statistics in the study there is convincing evidence that American Baptists tend to reject the sectarian mentality that views evangelism as simply preparing for heaven, and to give their greatest support to a view of evangelism which includes social transformation. One might criticize the Roper questionnaire in respect to these responses on the grounds that it did not allow sufficient alternatives to the questions on evangelism. The Roper questionnaire allows two choices for the support of evangelism which allowed an emphasis on the "social gospel" (no. 2 and no. 3) and only one choice for those who would have more conservative convictions (no. 1). This limitation may have biased the responses. Nevertheless, the results are significant (Roper, page 51):

Number of respondents	997
	%
1. Evangelism is the changing of an individual person to give him personal salvation without regard to his involvement in society. It's to get him ready to live in heaven	16
2. Evangelism is to create a new person in every relationship he has in the community and help him become a participant as a new person in all of these relationships	37
3. Evangelism is our work in God's plan to redeem and transform men and the forms and institutions of human society	45

All of them (volunteered)   3

None of them (volunteered)   2

Don't know   2

Some ministers have claimed that the social involvement of the denomination has alienated a supposed majority of the membership who cling to the belief that traditional evangelism is the primary task of the church. They claim that the program of the American Baptist Convention has changed too rapidly for its constituency and that people are upset with these departures from the former role of the church. However, if members are discontented with the increased social involvement of their denomination, the Roper statistics do not show evidence of such discontent. Actually, the overwhelming majority are either pleased with the Convention's attempt to keep abreast of the times or are claiming that it needs to be even more related to the pressing social needs and issues of the times. Only a small minority believe that the denomination is out of line in its attempts to achieve social relevance and would like to have a return to what they consider to be "the real work of the church." This is further evidence of a concern for this world which is a concomitant of middle-class standing (Roper, page 55).

Number of respondents	997
	%
The American Baptist Convention is way behind the times and needs drastic changes to bring it up to date	4
The American Baptist Convention is a little behind the times and needs some changes to bring it up to date	24
The American Baptist Convention has kept pace with the times and is where it should be for a church organization in today's world	41
The American Baptist Convention is moving a little too fast into new ways even for a church organization in today's world	7
The American Baptist Convention is moving much too fast into new ways and getting away from the real work it should be doing	8
Don't know	16

A consideration of social class factors may help to explain criticisms of the denomination which arise in many quarters. For instance, the American Baptist Board of Education and Publication is continually under attack from various sources because of its church school materials. The critics often claim that the church school curriculum of the American Baptist Convention is non-biblical or is theologically liberal. However, a careful objective evaluation of these materials will reveal that they are filled with biblical content and adhere to a theological position which is easily identified as conservative.

It may be that those who oppose the denomination's church school materials are unconsciously expressing a lower-class bias against publications which are too much oriented toward a middle-class constituency. The cultural values inherent in these materials, the level of education required of the teacher to utilize them, the subject matter, and the illustrations often express a middle-class tone. Undoubtedly, those of lower socioeconomic status would find such publications detached from their style of life and alien to their thinking. Their refusal of the denomination's materials on the grounds that they are unbiblical or liberal may thus be an expression of the cultural alienation they experience when dealing with these materials.

The cultural conflict between the predominantly upper-middle-class American Baptist Convention and those segments of the denomination which hold lower social status can have far-reaching consequences. It may be that the denomination as a whole will find it difficult to relate effectively to the black churches within its membership. The style of life represented by blacks who tend to be of lower socioeconomic standing may differ significantly from that represented by typical white American Baptists. This difference may serve as a barrier to unification and cooperation in denominational planning.

There have been some Baptist leaders who have hoped for a merger between the American Baptist Convention and the Progressive National Baptist Convention, Inc. Such plans are unlikely to be realized if the cultural differences between American Baptists and their Baptist brethren in Negro conventions are too great. Samuel Hill and H. Richard Niebuhr both contend that denominational mergers usually occur between groups with the same class identity. This being the case, a merger of the American Baptist Convention with the Disciples of Christ or the Presbyterians seems more likely than a merger with Negro Baptists.

The middle-class orientation of the constituency and program of American Baptists probably also will hinder them from developing a ministry among the lower-class inhabitants of the inner city. Some observers have claimed that the city is secular and that the old-time gospel is often irrelevant in this urban cultural milieu. However, it may be not the old-time gospel as much as the middle-class church style to which urbanites are unresponsive. The cities are filled with religious people, but they tend to reject the churches of the bourgeoisie and flock to those sectarian establishments (including "store fronts") which fit their class tastes. Perhaps American Baptists should realize that the lower classes who are trapped in the inner city have little affinity for the kinds of music, sermons, church school materials, and youth programs which have become typical of their denomination. It just may be that God is not dead in the downtown districts but simply finds middle-class religion an unsuitable vehicle through which to express himself.

What Harvey Cox describes as the disposition of the modern urban man refers to a sophisticated member of the elite who often commutes to the city from his suburban home. Yinger is probably closer to reality when he contends that the mentality of many inner-city inhabitants is similar to that of the American frontier inhabitants of a hundred years ago. The sectarian religious forms which won the West for Baptists and Methodists (but which they since have abandoned in their upward mobility) are probably functional with such people in the modern urban setting.

Surely the success in the inner city experienced by the Pentecostal sect groups with their gospel music and unsophisticated sermons should be sufficient evidence of this reality. When the poor who live in the heart of the cities refuse to darken the doors of many downtown American Baptist churches, it is not Jesus they are rejecting, but Bach, seminary-trained clergymen, formal worship services, and middle-class hymnology. They feel quite at home in the sectarian store-fronts where an "old-time religion" is preached with fervor and the people sing "Do Lord" to the strumming of guitars.

It may be that a middle-class denomination should confine its efforts to middle-class communities and serve the inner city simply by helping to finance the work of those sectarian religionists who seem to have an affinity for that setting. In any case the American Baptist Convention will probably have increasing difficulty ministering in the inner city, not so much because the people there are secular, but because the class-oriented character of the denomination makes it out of place.

At this juncture some readers may conclude that the future of the American Baptist Convention lies in a ministry to middle-class people in suburbia and rural districts. Undoubtedly every state secretary of the denomination is aware that the suburbs which are emerging with lightning speed around each of our great urban centers are "high potential areas." Yet, American Baptist churches do not fare as well there as do Presbyterian, Methodist, and Episcopal churches. Much to the chagrin of many a suburban Baptist pastor, the in-migrant Baptists to his community often join other denominations while the Baptist churches pick up very few members from these other middle-class denominational groups.

A reason for this phenomenon may be that those who are moving to new suburban communities are also moving up the socioeconomic ladder. Their move to suburbia is just one symbol of their improved status and they will undoubtedly desire others. Denominational affiliation is such a way of demonstrating one's social standing; membership in the "right" church is important.

It is no secret that there is an unofficial status hierarchy among denominations, by which the middle classes tend to be Presbyterians, Methodists, and Episcopalians — but not Baptists. Baptists thus seem doomed to identification with their lower-class origins. With respect to middle-class identification, the American Baptist Convention is a "Johnny-come-lately" denomination and lacks the prestige of those churches that are long-standing members of this class. New members in a suburban community who want to affirm their newly acquired higher status with "proper" church connections will have difficulty in meeting this need through the typical local Baptist congregation. Even upwardly mobile Baptists will want to demonstrate their new class standings through denominational affiliations. Thus, it is not surprising that the suburban American Baptist congregation not only will tend to fail to attract members from the three middle-class groups which are mentioned above, but probably will also lack the status credentials to attract even many of the Baptists who happen to be moving into the community.

Let us consider what the Roper study says about the reasons given by people from other denominations to explain why they join American Baptist churches. Perhaps a careful evaluation will suggest that these reasons may be the bases for losses to other denominations which exceed the gains which they provide for Baptists (Roper, page 77).

Number of respondents	997
	%
Previously belonged to another denomination	35
Major reasons for transferring to American Baptist Convention:	
Changed to husband's, wife's church	10
Moved to another town and former denomination had no church there	6
Joined after moving here (no further information)	2
Introduced to it by friends, relatives	5
Baptist Church has principles, policies to my liking	5
Converted by minister, preacher I heard	3

American Baptists are likely to lose at least as many members as they gain by having persons change denominational affiliation in order to agree with that of their marital partners. It is probable (although no statistics are available) that in upwardly mobile families the tendency would be for the mate who is from the denomination of lower status to be the one who would change membership. Baptists who marry Methodists, Presbyterians, or Episcopalians are more likely to join the denominations of their spouses than the spouses would be to join theirs. The 10 percent gained through marriages of Baptists to non-Baptists is probably more than offset by losses to higher-class denominations by the same means.

Of American Baptists who previously belonged to other denominations, 6 percent changed because they found themselves in communities where there were no churches of their former affiliation. The American Baptist Convention is a smaller denomination than its middle-class competitors and has fewer churches located in fewer towns. Therefore, it is likely that Baptists will lose members rather than gain them as a result of mobile persons being unable to find churches of their former affiliation in their new communities.

New members (5%) may come into Baptist churches out of other affiliations through the influence of friends and relatives, but once again it is as possible that Baptists will lose members in at least the same proportion via this means.

The polity and practices of Baptist churches may be an attraction to lure members from other denominations. But it is just as likely that those gained through this enticement (5% of the constituency) will be offset by those who leave the Baptist folds because other groups have what appear to them to be better styles of church life. This movement seems particularly likely in light of the fact that many Baptists openly express discontent with their denomination's present polity and practice.

There are many who suggest that the Convention does not really provide an effective means for reaching decisions and molding policy. They claim that it ends up being manipulated by a handful of executives who are unchecked by the constituency.[10] Others claim it is too loose an organization, requiring no commitment to a definitive theological stance.[11]

Often ministers claim that they would be more free to preach their convictions if they were subject to a bishop or presbytery rather than the will of the local congregation. Many Baptist clergymen transfer to other denominations because of this belief. Such discontentment, evident in the ranks, does not suggest that the American Baptist Convention will experience a net gain because its practices and polity are preferable to those of other middle-class denominations. All of the above seems to suggest that the 35 percent of the constituency which joins American Baptist churches from other affiliations will probably be more than offset by losses to other denominations, particularly those of higher social status.

Needless to say, empirical studies are needed to verify such claims. However, the facts which are available point to the fact that this Baptist group is not growing through additions from other denominations. According to the Roper study, most members of the American Baptist Convention have simply inherited the religious tradition of their fore-fathers. The statistics show that over one-half of the members (52%) reported that they had been in American Baptist churches for "20 years or more" or "all my life." The chart below provided in the study shows the length of membership reported by age groups (Roper, page 76):

	Total	18-34	35-54	55 and over
Number of respondents	997	178	438	381
	%	%	%	%
1 year or less	3	8	3	1
2 to 4 years	10	21	11	3
5 to 9 years	10	22	12	3
10 to 14 years	12	19	13	6
15 to 19 years	9	10	12	6
20 years or more	38	6	32	59
All my life (volunteered)	14	12	13	16
Don't know	4	2	3	6

Some may question whether a denomination which no longer has an affinity for the lower classes, yet lacks the image to attract those with a middle-class style of life, can long endure. As early as the 1950's, while other middle-class denominations were experiencing phenomenal increases in membership, there was evidence that the American Baptists were having a bad time. Denominational officials pointed out in 1957:

Each day since 1950, American Baptists have been losing 1.2 members per hour.

On each successive Sunday, during the past six years, there have been almost 201 fewer people in our membership. American Baptists have been losing 10,473 members each year. . . .
If the trend of the past six years continues, within a decade over 100,000 members and 500 churches will be lost.[12]

Undoubtedly, there are many factors influencing this condition, but class factors should certainly be considered as being among the significant ones. The lower classes are alienated from this increasingly middle-class denomination while it lacks the image to attract middle-class people. To lack a definite affinity for any specific socioeconomic sector in society is not an enviable attribute for any religious organization.

3

Who Are American Baptists?

IN ADDITION TO THEIR social class orientation, American Baptists need to be studied in light of racial, sectional, age, and sex representation.

The Race Factor

Blacks are represented in the membership of the American Baptist Convention in exactly the same proportion as they are represented in the general population of the nation (Roper, page 74).

	American Baptists	Estimated Census (7/1/68)
	%	%
White	89	89
*Non-white	11	11

*In this survey we found 0.4 percent who were of other races. In the Census 0.6 percent are classified as other. In breakdowns throughout this report those of other races are included in the category "non-white." Despite their inclusion, however, the "non-white" category is almost entirely black people.

47

However, one should not conclude from these findings that the churches of the denomination have experienced extensive racial integration. The racial balance within the American Baptist Convention is the result of the membership of black churches in the denomination, and does not necessarily indicate that blacks have become members of white churches in significant numbers. Unfortunately, the eleven o'clock hour on Sunday for American Baptists, as for most of Christendom, is still a highly segregated hour. White American Baptists have their churches while black American Baptists have theirs.

Efforts to integrate churches have been made by many white congregations, and these efforts have yielded some admirable results. However, white pastors often complain that though the doors of their churches are open for black members, few seem to come. The class factor may once again be significant. Many blacks would sense deep alienation in the middle-class church styles adopted by most white American Baptist churches. However, some middle-class blacks adjust quite well in the white middle-class churches and at times prefer them to the churches in the black community. The cultural difference between some lower-class blacks and the middle-class orientation of many white churches may be a greater barrier to integrating American Baptist churches than are the racial differences.

Integration of local churches might be achieved by white members becoming a part of black churches rather than the reverse which is commonly expected. Why should black churches lose members to white churches in order to achieve racial balance? It seems that the whites are willing to meet blacks on their own territory (i.e., the white churches). But whites are often unwilling to endure the insecurity of meeting the blacks on *their* territory (i.e., the black churches). They would no longer be playing the gracious role of accepting people of another race into their church, but would be in the shaky position of hoping to be accepted by their black brothers. Furthermore, the willingness to be pastored by a black minister would be a good test for prejudice in whites. White Christians often reveal their latent feelings by an unwillingness to accept black men as leaders of their churches.

Black members of the denomination seem to lack a deep involvement with American Baptist programs. Only 10 percent of them (compared to 44 percent of white members) had enough awareness of the American Baptist Convention to know that the national offices of the denomination were located at Valley Forge, Pennsylvania (Roper, page 69). A very small percentage of the black church members kept in touch with denominational news through the newspaper *Crusader* or the magazine *Mission* which the Convention was publishing at the time the survey was being conducted (Roper, page 23).

	White	Non-white
Number of respondents	885	112
	%	%
Ever read *Crusader*	67	32
Read monthly	45	8
Ever read *Mission*	24	21
Read monthly	10	6

The Secret Place, a publication which the denomination puts out to aid members in daily devotions, gets a slight reading among blacks (5% as compared to 38% among whites, Roper, page 37).

The Roper statistics seem to indicate that the black members of the American Baptist Convention are somewhat detached from what is going on within their denomination. This detachment of blacks from the life of the American Baptist Convention as evidenced in the Roper study can be attributed in part to the ministers. Some 42 percent of the black members claim that most of what they know about the denomination comes through their pastors. Add to this another 21 percent of these members who gain the information from their church bulletin — which in most congregations is composed or controlled by the pastor. Usually pastors wield more influence in black churches than in white churches. Thus, the effort which they put forth to communicate the denominational program to members is of crucial significance (Roper, page 18).

	Get most of news from:			
	Convention newspapers or magazines	Local minister	Church bulletin	Convention pamphlets
Race	%	%	%	%
White	36	27	20	14
Non-white	15	42	21	11

However, the alienation which the black members of the American Baptist Convention sense toward their denomination cannot be simply attributed to the failure of pastors to promote their denomination in their local churches. The Roper study shows that the Convention has a more negative image among blacks than it has among whites. Some 39 percent of the black constituency, compared with 27 percent of the whites (p. 56) contend that the Convention "is behind the times." They tend to show a greater dissatisfaction with the denomination's program than do whites (Roper, page 59).

	Completely satisfied %	Generally satisfied %	Bothered %
Total church members	34	39	23
Race			
White	34	41	22
Non-white	38	24	34

In sharp contrast to the white community, blacks tend to believe that the denomination places too little emphasis on civil rights and race relations (Roper, page 64).

	Civil Rights and Race Relations	
	Too much emphasis %	Too little emphasis %
Total church members	18	10
Race		
White	20	9
Non-white	7	22

This negativism toward the Convention is probably part

of the attitude which blacks tend to maintain toward the entire "white establishment." The denomination is likely to be identified with the power structures of society which have responded all too slowly to the requirements for racial equality and justice. The general attitude toward all religion seems to reflect such a disposition toward the dominant social institutions of America (Roper, page 48).

	Percent saying religion has less influence
Total church members	54%
Race	
White	53
Non-white	61

However, if black members are to identify more closely with the American Baptist Convention, their denomination undoubtedly will have to improve its image among them. This can best be done by more actively engaging in social action programs which will promote those ends which blacks deem essential to their human dignity.

The Sectional Factor

The Roper study shows that the membership of the American Baptist Convention is concentrated more in the Northeast and the Midwest than in the other two sections of the country. It should be noted that membership in the Far West is approximately equal to the proportion of the total United States population in that area (Roper, page 75).

	American Baptists	Estimated total population (7/1/68)
	%	%
Northeast	35	24
Midwest	36	28
South	11	31
Far West	18	17

Sociologists are well aware of the fact that each of these geographical sections of the country represents a distinct subculture which differs from the others. Values, attitudes, styles of life, and institutional structures show great variation when any one of these sections is compared with any of the others. The differences between these sections is tending to become more pronounced, as the contemporary political situation is beginning to reveal. President Nixon can count on substantial support for his policies in the Midwest, while the northeastern part of the country poses his greatest opposition. The conservatism of the Midwest, particularly in the rural areas, evidences an attitude toward such issues as race relations, the Vietnam war, and student unrest vastly different from that which exists in the liberal Northeast. Undoubtedly the differing moods of these two sections would also emerge in evaluations of religious ideas and denominational programs.

Some small evidence of the differing religious attitudes between the Northeast and the Midwest was acquired by the Roper associates when they surveyed attitudes toward "open membership" in Baptist churches. The figures below show the apparent northeastern liberalism with respect to receiving non-immersed persons into church membership, and evidences a midwestern conservatism on the same issue (Roper, page 53).

	Approve of transfer by letter	Accepted only if baptized by immersion
	%	%
Total church members	53	42
Geographic area		
Northeast	66	29
Midwest	44	49
South	45	52
Far West	50	44

Both of these geographical sections have about equally proportionate representation within the denomination, so that neither side possesses the dominant position necessary to enforce its preferences on the other.

Even as cultural differences which are reflected in religious beliefs and practices are demonstrable between the Midwest and the Northeast, so there are cultural differences among all of the other sections. One can only wonder how a denomination whose geographical boundaries encompass all of these sections can promote a program and formulate a policy which would be commonly accepted. Undoubtedly much of the conflict and difficulty within the denomination reflect sectional differences. Attitudes toward evangelism, Christian social action, and church school materials would be affected by this. Perhaps the American Baptist Convention as it is presently organized is endeavoring to do the culturally impossible. Increased support and participation might result if the denomination were broken down into smaller units each with its own indigenous program.

The Age Factor

The denomination consists of a much lower percentage of young people and a much higher percentage of older people than is characteristic of the nation. Almost two-thirds of the resident adult members are 45 years of age or older (61%), compared with 47 percent of the general adult population. The percentage of members in the 18-to-24 age bracket is particularly low (Roper, page 74).

Age	American Baptist adult resident members	Population of U.S. 18 and older (Estimates 7/1/68)
	%	%
18-24	5	17
25-34	12	18
35-44	21	18
45-54	23	18
55-64	17	14
65 and over	21	15

The youth are underrepresented in the membership of all major denominations. This may be because religion tends to serve a supportive function for the socioeconomic system with which young people seem increasingly disenchanted. Youth, more and more, are expressing a willingness to stand in opposition to the structures of society, claiming them to be unjust and oppressive. Religious institutions which are identified with a social establishment that is increasingly under attack by the prophets of the youth culture (e.g., Pete Seeger, Bob Dylan, and Joan Baez) can hardly gain in popularity within this segment of the population.

Another possible explanation for the loss of youth may be the fact that religion, to a significant degree, deals with problems of suffering and death. These are issues which may be somewhat unreal to modern American young people. Youth have little need for the concern of a theodicy to set personal tragedies in a meaningful context. In today's world they can expect long life and little suffering in comparison with earlier centuries. Thus, with respect to handling life's tragedies, religion is somewhat dysfunctional for them.

This observation might lead to the assumption that the church might become attractive to youth if it abandoned the tendency to provide a theodicy and became socially relevant. A church involved with the socioeconomic problems of this world might gain the support of modern young people who have little interest in a religion which simply prepares them for the next world. However, such an assumption is difficult to support in light of the empirical data provided by the Roper study. While it is true that the cohort between the ages of eighteen and twenty-four is most inclined to say that the American Baptist Convention is "behind the times," it is difficult to ascertain what they mean by the statement (Roper, page 56).

	The American Baptist Convention:			
	Is behind the times %	Has kept pace with the times %	Is moving too fast %	Don't know %
Total church members	28	41	15	16
Age				
18-34	36	49	8	7
35-54	32	41	14	13
55 and over	20	38	20	22

There is almost no evidence to support the claim that young people want their churches to function as instruments for social change. The Roper study does not substantiate the claim that they are uninterested in organized religion because of the failure of the church to become involved in societal issues such as race (Roper, pages 64, 60).

	Civil Rights and Race Relations	
	Too much emphasis %	Too little emphasis %
Total church members	18	10
Age		
18-34	12	16
35-54	20	11
55 and over	20	7

	Viewpoint on community problems	
	Church should be more involved %	Church too much involved %
Total church members	7	8
Age		
18-34	11	7
35-54	8	8
55 and over	5	.9

The explanation for their alienation from churches must lie elsewhere. Those who want to prod the church into social involvement by making the claim that such involvement is required as a condition for keeping young people in the church will find little support in these statistics.

Perhaps the explanation for the lack of interest in organized religion on the part of young people lies in the failure of the church to provide mystical experiences for its members. As American Baptist churches have become increasingly rationalized, they have discarded the emotionalism and ecstatic states which were so much a part of their earlier existence. The mystical relationships associated with personal conversions have been de-emphasized in order to make room for a religion which stresses social justice and progressive societal change.[18] The abandonment of the mystical emphasis of experiential religion may have left the contemporary generation with a feeling that organized Christianity has failed to meet its basic spiritual needs.

The growing fascination of young people for drugs may be symptomatic of a craving for religious ecstasy. The drugs provide a pseudo-religio-mystical experience that, when described, seems strangely akin to the accounts of conversion outlined in William James' book *The Varieties of Religious Experience*. Could it be that young people, failing to find an experiential type of personal relationship with transcendent reality within the church, have turned for fulfillment to chemically induced religious feelings?

The drugs would certainly fit the disposition of modern young people who, by their use, seek to achieve a religious Nirvana by a "scientific" means. LSD does not require acceptance of a hard-to-believe theology in order to work. To the sophisticated young person such drugs offer mystical sensations in a form that the positivistic thinker can accept. He can have religious feelings without having to think religiously. This possibility is attractive to those who find it increasingly difficult to subscribe honestly to Christian beliefs in the midst of a secular intellectual setting.

The craving for the mysterious religious experience seems basic to the nature of man. Dostoyevsky proclaimed this clearly in the myth of "The Grand Inquisitor."

> . . . man seeks not so much God as the miraculous. And as man cannot bear to be without the miraculous, he will create new miracles of his own for himself, and will worship deeds of sorcery and witchcraft, though he might be a hundred times over a rebel, heretic and infidel.[14]

How else can we explain the growing interest which young people express for the occult arts, astrology, and Zen? What other explanation can account for the soaring sale of Ouija boards to a generation reared on Einstein and astrophysics? It just may be that churches, "relevantly adjusted" to the scientific orientations of the age, have lost the capacity to provide ecstasy and mystery for a youthful generation which craves these experiences. Would it not be ironical if, in an effort to become "relevant" to youth via programs of social action, the church had lost the ability to meet the religious hungers of its young people?

What the Convention sometimes has considered religion, Soren Kierkegaard has called moralism. That famous Dane claimed that one must go beyond this ethical religiosity by means of a "leap of faith," and only such a subjective commitment to that which is deemed ultimate could provide deliverance from the anxiety of existence. In short, youth may find the main-line denominations unattractive simply because they do not offer conversion experiences.

It is interesting to note that while the Baptist Student Movement has been dissolved, groups such as Inter-Varsity Christian Fellowship and Campus Crusade are experiencing tremendous growth on most university campuses. Those groups which seem preoccupied with conversion experiences apparently flourish, while those which emphasize more "relevant" religious expressions seem to die. The American Baptist Convention experiences a loss of its youth while fundamentalistic sects, with their emotionalism, have a growing attraction for this same group.

The Sex Factor

It may not be surprising to learn that 63 percent of American Baptists are women (Roper, page 73). In the United States women generally have been more involved with institutionalized religious activities than have men. This factor is partly due to the fact that in our society women are primarily in charge of rearing the young. Religion is an important factor in this process of socialization, for it gives sacred support to the rules and values which women endeavor to have their children uphold.[15]

Another explanation for the greater interest in organized religion evidenced by females is related to their role expectations in the American society. They, more than men, are expected to abide by the ethical standards of the culture. Since our society connects ethics with religion, the females who are required to be the more moral of the two sexes are, consequently, expected to be the more religious.[16]

Finally, we must consider the fact that in America most

women have fewer secular-group contacts than do men, so that religious-group associations play a more important part in their lives. They are able to gain status in church activities whereas their opportunities for recognition are limited in many of the other institutions of society. Women who are forced into subordinate positions within most organizations can achieve positions of leadership within the church structure.[17]

The disproportionate representation of females in Baptist churches creates many problems. First of all, there is a shortage of eligible males for women who want to marry persons who share their religious convictions. Almost every Baptist pastor has tried to think of available partners for some attractive, dedicated unmarried women in his church, only to become more aware that unattached single men who are committed Baptists are rarities. Another consequence stemming from this situation is that churches have additional difficulty raising financial support. Contributions made by couples who are committed to the church far exceed those made by single women or by women whose husbands have no connections with organized religion.

Some social scientists have tried to make the point that women are innately more religious than men. The Allport-Vernon-Lindzey scale defines in behavioral terms many emotions and dispositions, thus allowing them to be quantitatively evaluated to some degree. Studies employing the scale indicate that females have a higher religious propensity than males.[18] Frederick Davenport makes the same claim but without empirical data in his classical work *Primitive Traits in Religious Revivals*.[19] However, these studies do not account for the fact that in many societies women are less prominent in religious activities than men. Among Muslims, Buddhists, and Jews, the men are usually more involved than the women with institutionalized religion, although some recent trends are changing this condition.

There is some evidence of a recent tendency toward convergence of attitudes of men and women with respect to religion. Among younger people in the population the differences between males and females with respect to religious interest seem to be diminishing.[20] Perhaps in the future, Baptist churches will not be attended predominantly by females as is the case today.

An additional item of interest is that, while females are the majority of the American Baptist membership, they are underrepresented in the leadership of the denomination. They represent a definite minority on the policy-making committees and among the executives and elected officials. Already the Women's Liberation Movement has had an impact on the life of the denomination through demonstrations at the Convention's annual meeting. The Division of Christian Social Concern, one of the few agencies of the denomination headed by a woman, has declared its intention of pressing for an end to the second-class status which allegedly women must endure within the life of the Convention. Imagine the ramifications of having the sexes represented in the leadership of the denomination in proportion to their membership! Could the American males, who already have their masculinity threatened by the prevailing cultural trends of the nation, cope with such a condition?

4

What Kind of Church Members Are They?

AFTER EXAMINING AMERICAN BAPTISTS in the larger context of society, let us look more closely at their participation in the activities of the local church.

They Support Morning Worship

According to the Roper study the members of American Baptist churches attend worship services with a high degree of faithfulness. Sixty-five percent of them claimed that they attend church once a week or more. An additional 12 percent said that they attend about twice a month and 7 percent reported that they attend once a month. (See table on page 63 of this book.) However, it may be that the Roper study failed to obtain an accurate description of church attendance because of some possible faults in the questionnaire. The interviewers asked the following (item 73 in the questionnaire):

> About how often do you attend worship service — once a week or more, about twice a month, about once a month, or less often than that?

61

Once a week or more
About twice a month
About once a month
Less often
Never (volunteered)
Don't know

Since there is often a tendency for respondents to portray themselves in the best possible fashion, the wording of the questionnaire may have allowed them to describe their ideal imagined selves rather than reality. Perhaps the truth might have been ascertained more accurately with questions such as these:

1. Did you attend church *last* Sunday?
2. Did you attend church the Sunday before last?
3. Did you attend church every Sunday in the past month?

When both of the above sets of questions were tested with a group of respondents, a significant proportion of those who claimed to attend worship once or more each week said they failed to attend the previous Sunday. Of course, they pleaded that the previous Sunday was an exception. Nevertheless, it is safe to assume that in such matters persons often think of themselves as more faithful than their actual behavior reveals. It is therefore preferable to get specific information about specific events which occurred on specific dates. The questions in the Roper study are too general to elicit the truth with precision.

In most Protestant denominations approximately one-third of the church members can be expected to attend worship on any given Sunday. American Baptist churches probably fare better than most others, because they claim to admit into membership only "believers" who personally decide to join these churches. This policy gives them a decided advantage over churches which practice infant baptism and therefore admit non-consenting children into their memberships. Obviously, the latter groups would have less of a possibility of maintaining faithfulness among their constituencies than would Baptists. Also, American Baptist pastors seem inclined to remove inactive members from their church rolls. Considering these factors, it may be that 50 percent is a figure more descriptive of the proportion of American Baptists who can be found in worship services each week (even this figure is somewhat optimistic). Nevertheless, the Roper study reports the following (Roper, page 78):

	Attend worship services				
	Once a week or more	About twice a month	About once a month	Less often	Never (volunteered)
	%	%	%	%	%
Total church members	65	12	7	15	2
Sex					
Men	70	13	5	11	1
Women	63	10	7	17	3
Age					
18-34	57	13	11	18	1
35-54	69	12	5	13	1
55 and over	65	11	6	15	3
Race					
White	05	11	6	16	2
Non-white	69	18	8	5	—
Educational level					
College	68	15	7	9	*
High school	63	10	7	19	2
Grade school	67	11	3	13	6

*less than 0.5%

In comparison to some other countries (e.g., England), the support which American Christians give to their churches seems astounding. American churches seem to be enjoying a period of relative prosperity just when the churches in Europe seem to have been deserted, in what some have called a post-Christian era. In one sense America has become more religious in the past few decades than it has ever been before. At present approximately 60 percent of the nation's population belong to religious organizations, compared to a mere 10 percent who held such membership at the time of this country's founding. Billy Graham may proclaim that America is straying away from God but, on the other hand, historians do not give a good report of the "faith of our fathers." Yet in spite of this increasing religiosity many feel that religion is less influential in our national life than during earlier periods of our history. Commenting on the contemporary era, Henry Steele Commager says:

> . . . though church statistics attain an unreliability that would be a penal offense in a corporation, it was apparent that church membership was growing more rapidly than population. The increase in wealth and in social activities was even more impressive; the churches, of necessity, borrowed the techniques of big business, and bishops were often chosen for their administrative talents rather than for their spiritual qualities.
>
> Never before had the church been materially more powerful or spiritually less effective. . . . The great moral crises of two world wars failed to elicit any authoritative religious leadership or even to inspire any spiritual interpretation, and not the clergy but the scientists instructed the American people in the moral consequences of the use of the atomic bomb.[11]

The Roper study empirically supports this statement, for it shows that while American Baptists tend to be faithful church members, the majority (54%) believe that religion has a declining influence in today's world. Only one-quarter of American Baptists say that religion has more influence, and 16 percent say it has about the same influence. Several key groups indicate that they think religious influence has lessened — younger people, the better educated, and black church members (Roper, page 48).

	Percent saying religion has less influence
	%
Total church members	54
Age	
18-34	59
35-54	57
55 and over	49
Race	
White	53
Non-white	61
Educational level	
College	58
High school	53
Grade school	50

Will Herberg attempts to explain this seeming contradiction of churches growing in wealth and membership while losing their influence upon society. He claims that people have turned to religious institutions over the past few decades because they find that within the American societal system religious affiliation has become a means of social identification. People in a former generation had identity ascribed to them on the basis of nationality; today, he says, they achieve identification through membership in religious organizations. Thus, whereas the first generation of immigrants gained a sense of belonging by claiming to be Polish, Italian, Irish, etc., the third-generation American meets the need to belong by claiming to be a Protestant, a Catholic, or a Jew. All other means of social identification are obsolete. The old ethnic identifications have been subsumed into the broader categories of religion. The various ethnic groups tended to merge, not into a single "melting pot" as earlier sociologists had predicted, but into what Ruby Jo Kennedy called a "triple melting pot." [22] Ethnic groups which had a Catholic background tended to merge. Those groups which had a common heritage in Protestantism formed still another unit for social identification. The Jewish ethnic groups did the same. Herberg states:

> Not to be a Catholic, a Protestant, or a Jew today is, for increasing numbers of American people, not to be anything, not to have a *name;* and we are all, as Riesman points out, "afraid of chaotic situations in which [we] do not know [our] own names, [our] 'brand' names. . . ." To have a name and an identity, one must belong somewhere; and more and more one "belongs" in America by belonging to a religious community, which tells one *what* he is. . . .
> On one level at least . . . the notable increase in religious identification, affiliation, and membership — is a reflection of the social necessity of "belonging," and today the context of "belonging" is increasingly the religious community. [23]

Peter Berger explains the material prosperity of churches during the recent past as a consequence of religion's abandoning its "prophetic" function for a "priestly" function. According to Berger the prophetic function is one in which the church pronounces the judgment of God upon the injustices and inequities of the society. Such pronouncements would inevitably render the church socially unpopular and it would then suffer in terms of a reduction in material support given by contributors and a marked decline in attendance at services.

Berger charges that the church, rather, has assumed the priestly function in which it provides an ideological justification for the social system and acts in a supportive role for "the establishment." A church which encourages the populace to regard the institutions of society (economic, political, educational, etc.) as ordained of God will inevitably define opposition to the structure of those institutions as a sin against the Almighty. Needless to say, when religion serves such a supportive and integrative function for society, it will gain broad support from all sectors of the population.[24] (Billy Graham may have come dangerously close to this in his observance of "Honor America Day," which was held on July 4, 1970).[25]

Berger claims that the church has encouraged people to adjust to the world as it is, to affirm the "O.K. World." The church has aided in socializing people into supporting the institutions and values of society. For its services the society has rewarded the church with increases in membership and material wealth. However, Berger bemoans this condition, for he says that such a church is unfaithful to its calling when it fails to respond to its obligation to pass its Christian judgment on the socioeconomic system which in many ways is evil.[26]

Perhaps J. Milton Yinger is correct when he suggests that Herberg and Berger may be bearing down too hard on the church in an attempt to explain the good support which American Christians customarily give to their religious institutions.[27]

In the light of these many criticisms, it seems as though the church is damned if it relates to the world and damned if it does not. If the church serves an integrative and supportive function for society, it is accused of "selling out to the establishment."

On the other hand, if it is not integrated with the cultural system, it is called "socially irrelevant." If the church enjoys a growing membership, improved attendance at worship, and economic prosperity, it is charged with having made these gains by "compromising with the world." However, if the church fails to grow in size and wealth, it is subject to the criticism that it is unrelated to the social system, uninvolved with contemporary power structures, and detached from secular reality. Thus it finds itself trapped between two undesirable alternatives.

Baptist churches could do some things to improve the attendance at services and the calibre of their members. First there is a tendency to baptize into membership many young people who have not made a commitment to Christ. To achieve the success goals of the American Dream, some pastors pressure young people to join the church when they have not yet made up their minds about the Christian life. Too often pastors who claim to be opposed to infant baptism immerse children who are seven or eight years of age. Although some such youngsters may be able to grasp the significance of salvation, perhaps a much larger proportion of them are not yet at a point where a Christian commitment means very much. Kierkegaard once asked, "How can you consider a youngster ready for the sacrament when you cannot trust him with a ten-dollar bill?" A somewhat similar question might be asked of those who would bring children into church membership and then construct church by-laws that deny them decision-making powers in meetings of the church and congregation until they have reached eighteen years of age.

The fact that Baptist churches are loosening up their requirements for church membership is further evidenced in the increased tendency toward open membership. The rigid stipulations for membership which were designed to insure the faithfulness of members are being relaxed in order to allow a greater number of persons to join Baptist congregations. It can be argued that such a change is essential if the Baptists are to compete successfully with other denominations in the recruitment of new members. Nevertheless, lowering the requirements for membership may have a negative effect on the percentage of the constituency which can be depended on to attend church services as faithful and loyal members. Another bad omen for Baptist churches is the evidence that the religious revival which brought the masses into the churches in earlier years has diminished in frequency and influence. In recent years most denominations have experienced a rise in membership but a decline in worship attendance. There is good reason to suspect that the healthy condition of Baptists with respect to church attendance may already have seen its best days.

They Participate in a Variety of Church Activities

Over half of those interviewed by the Roper Associates reported that they attend other church services or meetings "fairly regularly." Once again the formation of the questions which were utilized in the investigation leaves something to be desired. They were as follows (items 74 and 75 in the questionnaire):

Aside from regular Sunday worship services, do you ever attend any other church services or meetings fairly regularly?

Yes [ask next question]
No [skip next question]

What else do you attend?

Sunday church school
Men's group
Women's group
Youth fellowship
Midweek services
Workers' conferences
Schools of missions
Choir
Other (write in)
Don't know

The structure of these questions, like those relating to church attendance, may have influenced the respondents to portray themselves in an overly favorable manner. Thus, the statistics may be exaggerations of the actual situation (Roper, page 79).

	Percentage who report attending other church services or meetings %
Total church members	57
Sex	
Men	64
Women	52
Age	
18-34	51
35-54	62
55 and over	53
Race	
White	56
Non-white	62
Educational level	
College	67
High school	53
Grade school	48

Regardless of the questions which might be raised about these findings, anyone acquainted with the American religious scene would expect a high level of participation in church activities. Such things as youth groups, couples' clubs, Sunday church schools, and women's groups, are often what attract people into church membership. Few parents with teenagers would consider joining a congregation that did not have "something for the young people." Ronald E. Osborn says:

> A typical American conviction is that a church should not merely exist: it should have a "program." The activism of our nature tells us that a congregation is of little worth unless it is "doing things" and that every member ought to carry his share of these activities.[28]

Among those activities which American Baptists support, Sunday church school heads the list. Women's groups are second in support, and midweek services rank third (Roper, page 80).

Number of respondents   997

                                             %
Attend
Sunday church school   28
Women's group   19
Midweek services   16
Men's group   10
Workers' conferences   10
Schools of missions   7
Choir   7
Business, committee meetings   5
Youth fellowship   4

A higher percentage of women (30%) attend women's groups than men attend men's groups (26%). Of the total who attend women's groups, over half (52%) are 55 or older; 41 percent are between 35 and 54; and only 7 percent are between 18 and 34. However, women younger than 35 are often burdened with small children, a circumstance which makes participation in such a program difficult. The men's total does not have this heavy orientation toward the elderly, though its youngest group still has a low representation. Men 55 years of age or older make up 37 percent of those who attend men's groups, 53 percent are 35 to 54, and 10 percent are 18 to 34 (Roper, page 80). The lack of participation by a significant proportion of the youngest members studied is symptomatic of the church's overall failure to attract the young.

From the Roper study one might conclude that the men's groups are not very far behind the women's groups with respect to the support which they receive from the constituency of the denomination. However, most of the denomination's state executives would probably report that the men's groups in their areas are very poorly developed, while the women's groups seem to have a fairly high level of success and organization. One reason for this fact is that ministers' wives often give large amounts of time to women's activities so that their contribution often far exceeds what their often harried husbands can give to the men's organizations.

Some idea of how these groups compare can be gleaned from a survey made for some leaders of the New Jersey Baptist Convention. While the methodology of their investigation has many shortcomings, their results do provide some interesting insights for this discussion. When asked, "How well do you think your church is doing in the following activities?" New Jersey Baptists gave the following replies:[29]

	Well	Fair	Poor	Don't know	Number of respondents
Men's groups	36	38	46	51	171
Women's groups	104	44	6	40	194

Obviously, the women's work is doing much better than the men's work in that state. The same would probably be true of other states as well.

Many denominational officials and executives feel that the men's groups are obsolete. Such critics claim that people are no longer oriented toward separate activities for men and women. Such separation is alleged to belong to an earlier era. They say that in contemporary society people desire programs which will keep family members together. Consequently, "couples' clubs" might succeed where men's groups have failed.

The Roper study did not investigate the level of participation in couples' clubs. This omission is probably due to the fact that those who helped compose the question schedule were denominational executives, and there is no denominational agency for "couples' clubs." Since these leaders were undoubtedly interested in the programs which they promote, they tested for the support which the constituency gives to men's groups and women's groups (they maintain agencies for these groups) and failed to explore the support which is increasingly being given to the groups which may be displacing them.

Youth Fellowship

The Roper study examined the religious activities of American Baptists eighteen years of age and above. Consequently, the study excluded from consideration the age groups which would coincide with those for which the Baptist youth fellowship program is planned. The study did show that in the 18-to-34 group, 8 percent said they attended youth meetings. However, this figure ought to be discounted because even the participation of these persons is somewhat unusual, considering the fact that youth fellowship groups are created for junior and senior high young people.

The study referred to earlier, which was made among New Jersey Baptists, gives some evidence that youth groups are faring well in local churches. Over 55 percent of the respondents said that the Baptist youth fellowship programs in their churches were doing well, and 31 percent said fair. The actual returns from 185 persons on the question of how well the youth groups were doing in their local churches were as follows:[30]

Well	Fair	Poor	Don't know	Number of respondents
102 (55%)	58 (31%)	12	13	185

In comparison with the statistics on women's groups, which were taken from the same New Jersey study and cited above, the youth programs were evaluated as even more successful. That same study indicated that New Jersey Baptists considered only the Sunday public worship service more important to their churches than youth programs.

It is very unfortunate that the Roper study did not include a survey of young people under the age of eighteen, because it probably would have depicted the most vital area of activity in the life of most churches. In many respects the youth programs are the most highly developed. They are usually marked by such features as socials, rallies, hymn sings, service projects, study tours, camping programs, and Sunday evening discussion meetings.

A sizable minority of American Baptist young people attend denominationally sponsored camps where they are encouraged to become dedicated leaders for local churches. These camps provide a core of some of the most consecrated and earnest workers for Baptist congregations. It would be interesting to know approximately what percentage of the ministers, missionaries, and lay leaders of the American Baptist Convention received their impetus for Christian service from these summer camping programs. Undoubtedly, a large proportion of first-time decisions for Christ take place in such settings.

Several decades ago, mass meetings played an important role in the programming for Baptist young people. Christian Endeavor rallies brought hundreds of Baptist youth together with Christians from other denominational backgrounds. The Christian Endeavor society was one of the most vital ecumenical activities in modern America. However, as denominational boards developed separate programs and as the educational emphasis shifted to participation by young people, rather than the presentation of addresses by evangelists, these rallies lost their significance. Many Baptist state organizations sponsor annual youth conventions which, in some cases, approximate the earlier Christian Endeavor rallies. But, for the most part, the mass meeting is being abandoned for more intimate encounters.

The turning away from mass meetings might be one of the most serious mistakes which denominational program planners have ever made. Such a tendency is the result of contemporary educational theory which suggests that meaningful learning and edification can best occur in "dialogical relationships." The small-group fad, with its corollary "the buzz group," has gradually become dominant in the Convention's youth programming. The whole trend has reached a climax in the sensitivity-group movement which has produced both desirable and harmful results. Those who have been caught up in the movement away from mass meetings evidently have been unaware of some of the most significant sociological findings of Emile Durkheim.

One important discovery of Durkheim was that the collective rituals of mass meetings are essential for creating loyalty to a social movement and solidarity among the members of the movement. The euphoria generated by such mass meetings enhances the dedication of the participants to the movement which the meeting represents. Without collective rituals, group solidarity wanes, dedication diminishes, and the movement dies. Note what has happened, for instance, to the civil rights movement since the mass rallies have passed away and the people have ceased the litanies of "We Shall Overcome." The labor movement lost its dynamic when the union rallies ended. The antiwar movement needs a march on Washington from time to time if it is to stay alive. Sociologists are well aware of the essential value of mass rallies for any movement.

For those who are unacquainted with the significance of collective rituals performed by mass groups and do not have the time to read Emile Durkheim's book *The Elementary Forms of the Religious Life*,[31] a good look at the contemporary youth culture might provide the necessary education. The claim that mass meetings are dysfunctional in the modern social setting is difficult to maintain in the face of Woodstock. There a half million young people came together in a gathering that was not devoid of religious (though not necessarily Christian) qualities. Many of those who attended Woodstock relate descriptions of "conversions" in which they gained a new perspective on life. One young person commented to the author:

> You can't imagine how I felt. I was caught up in something that transcended me. All those people chanting together — the way we had all come for the same thing. I felt like we were all one. I wanted to love everybody there — share everything I had. And the neat thing was that everybody else seemed to feel the same way. Nobody that was there will ever be the same.

Some of the participants in that rock concert said a movement was born there that will take over America. They talk of a "Woodstock Nation" that will propagate the unity and freedom which the participants enjoyed.

The Woodstock concert has given rise to a multitude of similar get-togethers. The same "rituals" occur at each of them. These include the taking of drugs, making love, sharing material wealth, attacks on "the establishment," and proclamations for peace. The life style is reinforced at each mass concert: the solidarity of the participants is greatly enhanced, converts to the movement are made by the thousands — and all the time some of the "over 30" planners for church activities claim that mass religious rallies have had their day.

I participated in the antiwar moratorium held in Washington, D.C., in November, 1969. I can testify to the almost mystical effect that the rally had upon my psyche. As Pete Seeger had at least 500,000 people chanting, "All that we ask you — is give peace a chance," I felt an increasingly intense commitment to do something to end the Vietnam war. I sensed a unity with the other participants which was exhilarating. People gave me food to eat freely, as a sense of deep oneness among us encouraged everyone present to share whatever he had brought.

A group of people seated on the grass in front of the Washington Monument shared a common meal. In that group there were three nuns, two businessmen, seven long-haired college students, six students who were "straight" (i.e., who followed the life style of the social establishment), one rabbi, three Negroes, and two elderly women. They had become one. Caught up in the ritual and swayed by rhythmical chanting, they had discovered a unity which, all too often, the church has failed to duplicate. Durkheim's theory concerning rituals was validated in this case. The repetition of such gatherings in the months ahead would only revitalize what was born that cold November day.

It would be good for the program planners for youth in the American Baptist Convention to review their attitudes about mass meetings in light of the recent happenings in the youth culture. While small groups have their advantages, the young people increasingly are turning to the mass movements. Such mass rallies do not discount small-group encounters, but rather create emotions and commitments which give small groups vitality. It may be that the Youth for Christ rallies of the fundamentalist sector of Christendom create such loyalties and commitments as the American Baptist Convention must create among its youth if it is to survive.

Regardless of one's personal opinions on this matter, there is probably a consensus that research is needed on the subject. The Roper study is not sufficient to meet our needs on this subject.

Midweek Services

There are many ministers who claim that the midweek
services (usually prayer meetings) are the source of spiritual
dynamism for their churches. Countless homilies have been
delivered in order to stress the importance of such meetings.
Yet, there seems to be a general consensus that these services
are passing from the American scene. The assumption that
secular activities are drawing people away from weekday
church programs is widely accepted. Nevertheless, according
to the Roper study, the midweek services of Baptist churches
are able to gain the participation of approximately 16 percent of the membership. More men (20%) than women (14%)
claimed that they attended these meetings. The youngest
cohort in the study (18 to 34) had a much lower percentage
(10%) who attended than did the two older groups (18% each)
(Roper, page 81).

There may be some question raised by the leaders of these
midweek services as to whether the 16 percent figure for
participation is valid. Most clergymen complain that the
number of members who attend prayer meetings can be
counted on one's fingers.

Perhaps the seemingly high percentage of participants
cited in the study is further evidence of some weaknesses in
the Roper study. The questionnaire failed to explore how
often those who claimed that they supported these services
actually attended. The respondents may have imagined themselves to be more faithful to the midweek meetings than would
be empirically substantiated if the questions were phrased
differently. Possibly a good number of those who claimed
to be active in these services rarely attended.

On the other hand there is no need to be overly skeptical
about the Roper figures. In many churches the midweek
services have been revised in format so as to make them
more attractive. Some pastors have turned these meetings into
study groups in which theological discussion is carried out
on a level that goes far deeper than is possible with the
much larger Sunday morning crowd. Discussions of important
religious books, biblical exegesis, sensitivity sessions, forums

on community problems, experiments with artistic expression, and many other innovations have helped to revitalize midweek get-togethers by church people.

In recent years many pastors have claimed that the spiritual renewal derived from small-group encounters has been the most vital part of the church life for many of the members. In response to complaints that the Sunday morning worship services are too large and impersonal for deep religious encounters to occur, pastors across the country have initiated the organization of religious "cell groups" which are each composed of about ten persons. These groups, because of their intimacy, provide unique opportunities for honesty and openness between persons.

In some of these groups something akin to the group therapy patterns employed by many modern-day psychologists is approximated. These gatherings often achieve such levels of trust between the members that they dare to bare some of the deepest troubles of their lives. These problems of existence are explored, discussed in accord with Scripture, and made matters of prayer by all the members of the group. In the midst of an impersonal society which often requires its citizens to be "other-directed," such communal events are often cherished by the participants. They claim such a gathering provides an opportunity to remove the facades they usually wear, and enjoy the freedom of honesty about themselves without the threat of rejection. People often feel that if they honestly confessed their true natures to most people, they would end up being penalized for their openness by ostracism. However, the loving intimacy which they find in these small groups provides an atmosphere wherein they can dare to be truthful. The group covenants together to ensure acceptance under all conditions, and this Christian acceptance creates the freedom for truthfulness.

Although the Roper study points out that 16 percent of American Baptists attend midweek services, it does not explore the nature and purpose of these meetings. Such restructured midweek gatherings which serve a new set of social and personal needs may indeed be bringing about a rebirth of what seemed to be a dying practice.

Workers' Conferences

Only 10 percent of American Baptists have attended workers' conferences. The groups within the sample which had the highest attendance were the men (16%) and the college educated (16%). The groups with the lowest attendance were women (7%), people aged 18 to 34 (5%), and those in the lower-income group (7%) (Roper, page 81).

The Roper Associates did not indicate the nature of these conferences. The Board of Education and Publication of the American Baptist Convention sponsors training programs for Sunday church school workers and youth leaders. On the state level, conferences are promoted for deacons, trustees, and other workers in the churches. Music directors, fund raisers, leaders of women's work, and leaders of men's work all have conferences provided which can increase proficiency in their respective areas.

More and more local churches are conducting day-long conferences at least once a year which bring together all of the leaders of the congregation in order to plan the programs of the church for the following twelve months. In this way the activities of each church are coordinated in such a way as to make them mutually supportive. The programs gain unity and the leaders gain an awareness of the many facets of the church life which they might not have realized otherwise.

A recent emphasis of the Department of Evangelism Planning of the American Baptist Convention may result in new and different kinds of workers' conferences. Some of the leaders in this organization have advocated a theology which calls upon the church to participate actively in social change. These leaders maintain that God wills that the church should be an agent of social change in each sector of the social system. They claim that in addition to working for the conversion of "lost souls," the church should also endeavor to convert the various institutions of society so that they will function under the lordship of Christ.

If this latter objective is to be realized, then the laity will have to be trained to accomplish the task. The laity live and work in these various institutions and social sectors which need to be restructured according to the will of God. Consequently, lay people must be trained so that they will know how to be agents of change and will sense what changes they should seek to bring about. Those who advocate this theology think that the church should set up training programs so that laymen can learn how to fulfill God's mission in all parts of the social system. Paul L. Stagg's book *The Converted Church*[32] and Jitsuo Morikawa's monograph *Pastors for a Servant People*[33] advocate that the church provide conferences which would prepare the laity to be the means of transforming those areas of life outside the religious sector where men spend most of their time.

In order to grasp some of the importance of what Morikawa and Stagg are suggesting, it would be worthwhile to turn to what many of those in the field of the sociology of religion have to say about modern trends of secularization. Scholars in this discipline claim that prior to the modern era all institutions enjoyed the sanctification of religion. The people believed that each of the institutions of society had its particular function and structure because God had ordained it so. Kings ruled because God willed them to these positions, and their laws were considered to be extensions of God's law. Those who broke such laws had done more than violate the dictates of the state – they had taken a stand against the ordinances of God (Romans 13:1-3). Likewise, the economic institutions were thought to be willed by God so that those in business and commerce were regulated by divinely inspired rules. So it was for each and every institution within the social system. God had ordained the establishment of each of them to serve mankind according to his desires.

Within such a social system the church played a dominant role. All was religiously prescribed and nothing lay beyond the vale of religious jurisdiction. This kind of society was sacred in its entirety. The church was socially involved and was able to express its values and orientations in every social sector. However, the sacred society did not last. Secularization began to make an impact upon this religiously defined system, beginning in the area of economics.[34]

Those involved in commerce and industry gradually detached their activity from church control. To reap the greatest profits and to develop modern capitalism, the styles of procedure laid down by the church had to be abandoned. For instance, the church's condemnation of usury was not conducive to the development of a capitalistic economy. A rational economic system required freedom from religious control.[35]

Interestingly enough, the Judeo-Christian cosmology provided the rationale for this essential freedom. Within the theology of Judaism, God was depicted as transcending man and his world, rather than being immanent within these historical entities. Such transcendence allowed man the freedom to be an individual and to participate in molding his own destiny. Man's ability to fashion an economic system along rationalistic lines was within his divinely ordained prerogatives. He could develop a system of industry and commerce marked by increasing efficiency — and increasing profits — in freedom. He believed that God had willed for him to use his own ingenuity to create such a rational economy, and it was not the right of the church to dictate policy in this area.

The rationalizing tendencies of Judaism were interrupted by the birth and development of Catholicism. The sway which the Roman church held over the socioeconomic activities of men reversed the trend toward a rational capitalistic economy which had been evident in the Jewish state. The Catholics brought the doctrines of the immanent presence of God to the fore, and Christendom came to believe that God was in everything and that everything should be regarded as sacred (i.e., under the control of the church).

However, the Protestant Reformation once again brought the Western world out of this sacred consciousness and gave a rebirth to the tendency toward rationalization. The Reformers condemned the "magical" imagination which perceived spirits and demons inherent in the empirical world. They once again affirmed the "totally other" transcendence of God and, consequently, recreated the necessary intellectual climate for the exercising of the kind of freedom in which the development of modern capitalism could occur. Economics became secularized; that is, it was considered beyond ecclesiastical control and part of "the world."

The church was to exercise authority in only religious matters, and what were considered religious matters were becoming fewer and fewer in number. The secular economy required a secular state to serve its purposes; so gradually the government was removed from control of the church. The rhetoric about "a nation under God" notwithstanding, the rational state was increasingly viewed as a creation of man rather than an establishment under God. One by one the other social institutions followed the trend and the sacred society of the middle ages came to an end. Peter Berger states:

> The logical development of this may be seen in the Lutheran doctrine of the two kingdoms, in which the autonomy of the secular "world" is actually given a *theological* legitimation.[36]

The church has been gradually shut out of most of the sectors of society. The arts, the courts, the government, the economy, and the educational system have each slipped away from ecclesiastical control. Only the family remains within the jurisdiction of religion. The family, which has become increasingly fragile under the impact of urbanization and industrialization, needs the support of the church to survive. Religious justification for its continued existence is essential in the face of many critics who claim the family to be a dysfunctional institution in the modern world.[37] Thus the church finds itself confined to delivering sermons on "Christian Family Life" and expected to remain silent about the activities in the other societal institutions. Therefore, it is not surprising to find that the church knows how to function successfully only in residential areas where family life is lived. The church has become detached from those sectors of the world where men earn their wages, where economic power is wielded, and where political decisions are made.

Most of the leaders in the Department of Evangelism Planning believe that the church must go back into those areas of society from which it has gradually become excluded. Since sociology has demonstrated that man is basically molded by the social system in which he lives, then the system must be Christianized if man is to become Christian in his daily life. The arts, politics, education, industry, commerce, and education are all decisive in the molding of the personalities of any culture. A church that remains uninvolved with these institutions will find that its people are socialized and influenced by non-Christianized social forces. If man is partly a cultural product, then the church should be concerned with all aspects of the culture that helps create him. The church should be committed to insuring that all the social institutions will treat man in such a manner that his God-given dignity is enhanced and the values of the biblical tradition affirmed.

Presently the church is not training its laymen to know how to transform the social structures into Christianized units, nor is the church even significantly aware of what a Christianized social system would be like. There is a need for conferences which would bring together laymen on the basis of their major life involvements so that they might explore the possibilities of transforming their particular spheres of activity into what God would have them be.

Those in the Department of Evangelism Planning foresee teachers coming together to ascertain what God would desire in the educational system and what can be done to bring his will into reality, businessmen meeting in order to determine what changes in the economic system would make it more Christian, and politicians coming together so that they might transform government according to Christian values and decide how to use political power for positive social change. If the denomination follows this direction, then such workers' conferences would become the primary activity of the church. Instead of 10 percent participation in workers' conferences the percentage would be significantly higher. The church program would be structured to prepare the laity for the mission of Christian social change in "the world."

Whatever the value judgments one may place on this tendency, the sociological description of the movement of the social institutions beyond the influence of the church is difficult to deny. If the gospel is to be "proclaimed in *all* the world," then the church must prepare its laymen to go back into those sectors of society in which its influence has been gradually minimized and there become agents for Christianization. The alternative is for the church to confine its activities to a shrinking religious sphere and write off the rest of the social system as being secular. This latter alternative would doom men to living in a society which, for the most part, could be labeled as post-Christian. Workers' conferences of a new kind may be the hope of the church.

Schools of Missions

A mere 6 percent to 9 percent of the membership of the American Baptist constituency have attended schools of missions (Roper, page 81). These programs, usually held in local churches on four consecutive Sunday evenings, are planned to inform the members about missionary work which is being carried out by various church agencies, especially the American Baptist missionary societies. The approach has been educational and the sessions have been structured to enable people to learn the facts and figures connected with the denomination's work at home and abroad. However, facts and figures have always been dull material and the schools of missions have consequently suffered.

There are many who claim that there is no substitute for a personal presentation by the missionary himself and that the denomination will never attract support for its projects unless the individuals who carry on the work confront church members personally with needs of missions. Time and again the criticism has been that it is easy to get support for missionaries whom congregations can get to know on an intimate basis, but difficult to gain interest in a program which presents the mission of the church in a more generalized fashion.

Such points of view may be quite valid, but it is physically impossible to have missionaries visiting all the local churches in order to promote their work. There are hundreds of American Baptist congregations and only a very limited number of missionaries. If these missionaries were to do the deputation work which some desire, they would spend very little time on the field. While many independent missionary groups are able to send speakers to churches upon demand, consideration should be given to how these activities have detracted from the speaker's primary purposes. There are missionaries from some "faith" mission boards who are home from the field doing deputation work every other year. There is some question about the effectiveness such persons are able to maintain on the mission field when the vast amount of time used for promotional activities is considered. Nevertheless, because of the availability of such non-denominational missionaries, American Baptist congregations have often invited them to speak in their churches. Such congregations often end up financially supporting these "independent faith missionaries" whom they know rather than the denominational missionaries who for them remain impersonal.

The question seems to be: "Do American Baptists want their missionaries on the field propagating the gospel or do they want them at home inspiring support from local congregations?" The denominational leaders have chosen the former course and have endeavored to use such means as the schools of missions to elicit enthusiasm for their projects. Needless to say, their hopes have not been realized. The percentage of younger people who are possible candidates for missionary service are almost untouched by this approach. (Only 3 percent of those in the 18-to-34 age bracket are attracted to schools of missions.) Over the last few years the financial support for missionary work has declined so that the denominational leaders are faced with the possible necessity of recalling some of their personnel from the field. The problem is too serious to ignore. A more effective means for missionary promotion must be devised. The Roper study suggests that the schools of missions have failed.

Sunday Church School

The Sunday school was not organized in the United States, but it has flourished in this country as in no other place on the globe. Because of the American doctrine of separation of church and state, the youth could not be religiously educated in the public school system as in some European countries. Also, the distribution of the population over this expansive nation resulted in the establishing of some small communities which could not support a minister. However, these communities could maintain Sunday schools, and such institutions sprang up across the continent. Often these Sunday schools were the foundations upon which churches were later developed.

In many instances the Sunday school was the primary means of evangelism. Children who had not become Christianized often were brought to Sunday school by concerned neighbors and thus introduced to the gospel message. Nowadays some churches have buses that go through neighborhoods picking up children who might not otherwise get to church. There may be much sarcasm and criticism leveled at the endless contests promoted by Sunday school superintendents in order to improve attendance rates, but the critics will never know how many people became acquainted with Jesus because of such devices.

There were instances where the Sunday school, though functioning in the same building, was somewhat independent of the church. People who were a part of the one were not always a part of the other. The need to view the Sunday school as a teaching arm of the church and to impress the relatedness of the two institutions led to some significant changes. Gradually the American Baptist Board of Education and Publication developed a carefully worked out curriculum which not only educated persons in biblical knowledge but also provided historical and doctrinal material in their denominational tradition. The name "church school" began to replace the name "Sunday school" and little by little the earlier dichotomy between the two organizations was overcome.

The Sunday church school tradition is still very much a part of the lives of many American Baptists. The Roper Associates report that attendance at Sunday church school remains close to 28 percent of the membership in each of the major age groupings. The exceptions are the college educated (35%), the black church members (20%) and the lower economic group (18%) (Roper, page 81).

Some black churches have not put the emphasis on Christian education programs which has been evident in white churches. This difference is reflected in the statistics. Also, in accord with an earlier statement, some of the materials written for Sunday church schools may be too representative of life in white Anglo-Saxon suburbs to be attractive to inner-city blacks.

The lower economic groups are generally less active in community associations than are the middle classes.[38] Their comparatively low level of participation in Sunday church school probably reflects this general characteristic. A large proportion of lower-class children are probably sent to Sunday church school in their early years, only to drop out of the organization when they reach the teenage period. This is the pattern for the lower classes.

The failure of the Roper Associates to collect statistics on those under eighteen years of age results in a somewhat limited presentation of the reality which exists in most Sunday church schools. In most churches those under eighteen make up the major proportion of those engaged in this area of Christian education. Probably the inclusion of younger people would have demonstrated that attendance at Sunday church school equals, or even exceeds, the attendance at morning worship.

5

How Much Do American Baptists Know About Their Denomination?

THERE HAS BEEN A GREAT DEAL of controversy over the programs which the leaders in many denominations have developed for their local churches. Specifically, many people have claimed that the American Baptist constituency holds a much more conservative set of beliefs than is implied in the printed materials and suggested activities which come from their national offices at Valley Forge, Pennsylvania. Hardly any of the American Baptist executives have escaped the barrage of criticism which often condemns the organization as being "rank liberal" in its theology and having a distorted overemphasis on social issues in its planning.

With respect to the denomination's program, leaders receive far more letters of condemnation than letters of praise. These leaders need to be aware that such negative reactions to denominational programs are not representative of the opinions of most American Baptists. However, these leaders doubtless often wonder if they are running so much against the main stream of thinking within the Convention that their programs will have detrimental long-range consequences for their denomination. The incoming letters probably suggest that the constituency wants the "old-time religion" with its traditional emphasis on personal evangelism. The executives must sometimes be tempted to give in to what the letters demand and keep peace within an already troubled organization.

Added to the dissonant letters are the protests which come from the state executives. These workers are in close contact with local pastors and are sensitive to the complaints about the denomination's possible overemphasis on the "social gospel." To many of them the discussions on race relations, poverty, and social justice have pushed traditional concerns of the church from available consideration. The emphasis on these social issues is said to have created divisions in local congregations, to have been used as justification for cutting back on contributions to the denomination's Unified Budget, and to have caused dissatisfaction at the "grassroots" level. In comparison with state executives, the executives on the national level are alleged to live in ivory towers of detachment from the members in the local churches and consequently to be unaware of how deeply the dissatisfaction with denominational programming runs in the constituency.

One state executive told me that he was tired of "putting out the fires which the Valley Forge people are continually starting." Another was not hesitant about explaining that he protected the American Baptists in his state from the national program. Those parts of the program which he thought would be offensive to the vast majority of the Baptists in his state were simply not passed on to the local churches. One pastor who was not in agreement with the views of this particular state official said, "He keeps the stuff he doesn't like locked up in a special closet in the state office. We have to go directly to Valley Forge if we want to get in on the total national program." ·

It is not uncommon for the leader at the state level to call the pastors of his region together in order to still the trouble which the national program has apparently caused. Surely, such conditions must cause apprehensions among the national executives and lead them to question whether or not they have gone too far in their emphasis on social action.

At this point we would be wise to consider the results of

the Roper study. The findings show some interesting contradictions to the above assumptions and allegations. In spite of the letters of criticism, the complaints from state executives, and the protests from local pastors, the sociological realities are: (1) that there is broad support for the program of the denomination; (2) that the emphasis on social involvement is fairly well received by the constituency; (3) that the convention is not moving "too fast" for most church members in respect to social involvement; (4) that the constituency tends to reject concepts of evangelism which do not include the redemption of the social order; and (5) that denominational leaders are generally respected.

The Roper Associates asked their respondents to express their overall feelings about the American Baptist Convention. They were shown a card with five statements that ranged from "completely satisfied" to "very bothered." In response 73 percent of the members claimed to be either "completely satisfied" or "generally satisfied" with the denomination. Only 23 percent expressed some degree of dissatisfaction. Of the dissatisfied group only a very small proportion were "very bothered" by the way the American Baptist Convention functions (Roper, page 58).

Number of respondents	997
	%
I am completely satisfied with the American Baptist Church the way it is	34
I am generally satisfied with the American Baptist Church, although there are things that bother me	39
I have mixed emotions about the American Baptist Church — there is a lot I like about it, but there is a lot that bothers me	17
There are some good things about the American Baptist Church, but there is a lot more I'm bothered by	3
I find I'm very bothered by the way the American Baptist Church is today	3
Don't know	3

When the sample was broken down into the various subgroups, some differences in the degree of satisfaction became evident. Those who were the most "bothered" by the denomination were men, young people, black church members, and the better educated (Roper, page 59).

	Completely satisfied %	Generally satisfied %	Bothered (Total — last 3 statements) %
Total church members	34	39	23
Sex			
Men	28	43	26
Women	38	37	21
Age			
18-34	28	41	29
35-54	28	44	26
55 and over	45	33	18
Race			
White	34	41	22
Non-white	38	24	34
Educational level			
College	19	48	32
High school	36	40	22
Grade school	61	18	14

Other empirical data in the Roper study show that these groups were dissatisfied because they thought that the American Baptist Convention was not "keeping up with the times" with respect to the demands of the modern social situation.

Those who responded that they were not "completely satisfied" with the denomination were given an open-ended follow-up question in which they were encouraged to express freely what it was that disturbed them. There was a wide range of answers given but only two gained slightly more than a 6 percent response. These two answers showed that those who were "bothered" fall into diametrically opposed camps. Of these respondents, 7 percent complained that the denomination should be more involved in community problems, while 8 percent complained that the denomination was too much involved in community problems (Roper, page 59).

From a statistician's point of view these groups of "bothered" members arc too small to provide any empirical basis for ascertaining the major causes for dissatisfaction which exist within the denomination. Nevertheless a breakdown of these two groups is given because they may present some interesting grounds for speculation (Roper, page 60).

	Viewpoint on community problems	
	Church should be more involved	Church too much involved
	%	%
Total church members	7	8
Sex		
Men	7	8
Women	7	8
Age		
18-34	11	7
35-54	8	8
55 and over	5	9
Race		
White	7	9
Non-white	8	3
Educational level		
College	14	11
High school	5	7
Grade school	1	4
Over-all feelings about American Baptist churches:		
Generally satisfied	12	10
Bothered	10	17

In relation to the question of how the members of the American Baptist Convention react to the denomination's emphasis on social issues (such as race relations) the Roper study provides some interesting figures. First of all, 43 percent of the respondents said that civil rights and race relations should be one of the major concerns of the denomination (Roper, page 62). This was equal to the proportion of the membership which thought that foreign missions should be a major denominational concern. Hence, American Baptist leaders have some empirical evidence that race relations is an area which American Baptists deem worthy of religious concern.

There is some suggestion in the Roper statistics that the emphasis on foreign missions may be as significant a cause for discontent with the denominational programming as is the emphasis on civil rights. These two areas were the most cited by respondents as having been subject to "too much emphasis" in the American Baptist program. However, a redeeming consideration for the emphasis on race relations is that 10 percent of the respondents answered to the contrary and said that too little emphasis had been placed on this issue. Foreign missions did not fare so well, as only 4 percent thought that too little emphasis had been given to this facet of the denomination's program (Roper, page 63).

	Giving too much emphasis	Giving too little emphasis
Number of respondents	997	997
	%	%
Named one or more activities	42	62
Civil rights and race relations	18	10
Foreign missions	17	4
Christian education	1	15
Home missions	2	15
Evangelism	3	13
Schools and colleges	4	11
Theological education	2	4
All of them (volunteered)	*	*
None of them (volunteered)	35	15
Don't know or no answer	23	23

*Less than 0.5 percent

These figures seem to be further evidence of the failure of those entrusted with the task of promoting foreign missions to impress the constituency with the importance of this dimension of the work of the denomination. The Roper study shows an interesting change in the order of priorities which now exists for American Baptists. Early in their history, foreign missions probably would have been of primary concern to them. In this report Christian education, home missions, and evangelism earned greater support for consideration as a major denominational concern than did foreign missions. Only support for schools and colleges and theological education ranked lower than foreign missions on the priority list developed in the study (Roper, page 62; page 30 of this book).

In addition to the poor promotional system of the denomination, another reason for the comparatively weak showing for support for foreign missions may be related to some widely held misconceptions of the results of foreign missionary work. Following the kind of mentality which is evident in some of James Michener's novels, many Americans have come to believe the myth that missionaries are clumsy people who are responsible for the cultural disruption of hitherto idyllic primitive cultures. Such Americans live with the misconception that some societies untouched by Western culture are composed of people who are happy "just as they are."

Naively, such critics of missionary programs ask, "Why carry to them our guilt and anxieties? Is our way of life superior to the simple ways of such natives? Are we not expressing ethnocentricism when we try to evangelize such tribes? Isn't their way of life best suited for them?" They imagine some idyllic Eden being ruined by missionaries who impose Victorian ethics and competitive American life styles on hitherto unspoiled primitives. Consequently, they think that it might be better if we solved our own problems in America before we try to change the rest of the world.

Such a rationale demonstrates a lack of anthropological sophistication. Most primitive societies are marked by practices of slavery, severe exploitation of women, and short life expectancies. Although modern types of guilt and anxiety are relatively unknown to the primitive, he lives with a fear which modern man can never comprehend. To the primitive, the world is invested with demons, witches, and souls of the dead, all of which threaten his existence. He fears curses placed on him by enemies, and trembles at the prospect that he may have inadvertently offended some unknown spirits. He probably believes in a good God who transcends this world, but he usually thinks of this God as detached from his predicament and unconcerned with his welfare. Most primitives believe that they are surrounded by evil beings who threaten their lives and that from these beings there is no deliverance.

It is about time that American Baptists become aware of the tragic condition of those who live in most primitive cultures. Too much of the literature about missions fails to depict the horrors of living in an unchristianized society. In spite of the claims to the contrary, many anthropologists are not convinced that primitive Africa was a happy place in which to live. As long as American Baptists are unaware of what life is like in a society that has not experienced the transforming power of Christianity, foreign missions will fail to be a top priority with them. The contributions of Christianity to western culture have too often been taken for granted.

Those of the Michener mentality usually ignore what would have happened to such primitive cultures as existed in the Pacific if the missionaries had not gone with their gospel of love. By any stretch of the imagination these islands would not have been left alone. Because money could be made by exploiting them as colonies, western culture, as represented by capitalistic interests, certainly would have gone to them even if missionaries had not. There is little question that the results for the natives were vastly superior when their first contact with the modern world came through Christian missionaries rather than through commercial interests. The foreign mission cause has been hindered by some erroneous propaganda and the promotional people should set the story right.

The failure of the denomination to create a concern for missions among its members was demonstrated by the fact that very few even knew where in the world American Baptists were working. Only a very small proportion of the respondents to the Roper questionnaire were able to identify from a list of countries those in which missionaries from the Convention were serving. Only nine countries received recognition from as much as 10 percent of the constituency (Roper, page 67).

Number of respondents	Total 997
	%
Named one or more countries:	73
Congo	35
India	31
Japan	19
Burma	16
Thailand	16
United States	13
Philippines	13
Africa	12
Haiti	10
Mexico	9
Hong Kong	8
Puerto Rico	6
South America	5

The prevailing ignorance of what American Baptists are doing on the foreign mission fields is reflected in the constituency's lack of willingness to support such ventures. When American Baptists were asked which causes they were most likely to support, overseas missions did not fare well (Roper, page 65).

	Most likely to contribute to	Least likely to contribute to
Number of respondents	997	997
	%	%
Relief for disaster victims	48	8
Christian education	47	3
Overseas missions	37	23
Inner-city missions	31	12
American Baptist colleges and seminaries	27	13
Starting new churches	23	26
None (volunteered)	2	13
Don't know or no answer	2	14

Two-thirds of the respondents (67%) claimed that home missions were of greater importance than foreign missions. More than one-fifth (21%) said that both kinds of missions were of equal importance, and only 11 percent said that foreign missions were the most important (Roper, page 67).

Getting back to the consideration of the attitudes of American Baptists toward their denomination's emphasis on social issues, only 15 percent of the membership thinks that the Convention endeavors to move too quickly in these matters. Those who plead for gradualism, and claim that the leadership is imposing upon them social concerns and viewpoints for which the local church members are not ready, will find little justification in the Roper figures. In attempting to demonstrate how American Baptists regarded their denomination's relevancy, the study showed the following (Roper, page 56):

	The American Baptist Convention			
	Is behind the times %	Has kept pace with the times %	Is moving too fast %	Don't know %
Total church members	28	41	15	16
Sex				
Men	36	36	15	13
Women	23	44	15	17
Age				
18-34	36	49	8	7
35-54	32	41	14	13
55 and over	20	38	20	22
Race				
White	27	42	15	16
Non-white	39	39	11	11
Educational level				
College	42	34	14	10
High school	24	44	15	18
Grade school	12	49	19	19

There is much in these figures to indicate that the Convention may be a trifle too conservative with respect to the desires of the membership and that its leaders should more energetically address themselves to relating the churches to the vital needs of the socioeconomic order.

The Roper study seems to suggest that the denomination's constituency has a much broader view of the work of the church than many conservatives have assumed. For instance,

American Baptists tend to hold a view of evangelism that includes the transformation of social institutions and restructuring of the social order. The respondents were shown a card with three different descriptions of the meaning of evangelism and asked which one came closest to describing what evangelism meant to them. The first statement represented a more conservative viewpoint on evangelism, and the other two more broadened viewpoints (Roper, page 52).

	To give personal salvation	*To create a new person in every relationship*	*To redeem and transform men and forms and institutions of society*
	Evangelism is:		
	%	%	%
Total church members	16	37	45
Educational level			
College	13	47	42
High school	15	33	50
Grade school	25	28	38
Frequency of worship service attendance:			
Once a week or more	14	38	47
Once or twice a month	19	39	45
Less often or never	19	32	42

Only minor variations appeared in the various subgroups of the sample. Men and women tended toward agreement, as did people in the various age groupings. Black members were like white members in the proportion of support given to each of the positions. The broader view of evangelism was held by the well educated while the poorer educated were more narrow in their positions. The less active with respect to church activities the respondents were, the more likely they were to hold the narrowest views of evangelism. This suggests that the critics of the denomination's social involvement tend to be those who are not supportive of their local churches. Those who are the supporters of the local church programs indicate a surprisingly high degree of backing for the belief that evangelism includes the transformation of the forms and institutions of society.

Perhaps the negative criticism of the denominational leaders for their strong emphasis on social involvement represents the opinion of a vocal minority while the "silent majority" of the American Baptist constituency is supportive of the positions their leaders have taken. The Roper figures should provide some basis for these executives to regard more lightly those many letters of protest which come across their desks.

Actually the Roper study gives some evidence to substantiate a claim that there is little significant criticism of the leaders from the members. When asked to pick from a list of characteristics which might describe the national leaders, the respondents made largely favorable choices. The leaders were thought to be conscientious, hard working, leading the Convention in the right direction, forward and progressive, closely in touch with the desires of church members, and holding views very similar to the majority of church members on religious matters (Roper, page 72).

	Total church members
Numbers of respondents	997
	%
Hard working	40
Conscientious	38
Leading the American Baptist Convention in the right direction	28
Forward and progressive	25
Closely in touch with the wishes and desires of church members	23
Has views very similar to the majority of church members on religious matters	22
Out of touch with the wishes and desires of church members	9
Has views that are too different from the majority of church members on religious matters	8
Too liberal	6
Too conservative	4
Behind the times	3
Leading the American Baptist Convention in the wrong direction	3
None	2
Don't know	28

These figures are somewhat surprising to a sociologist. Previous studies have led social scientists to believe that the leadership of any denomination is more liberal in theology and social perspective than the constituency.[39] Also, the carping criticism from dissonant sectors of the denomination has led many to believe that the "bureaucrats at Valley Forge" are out of touch with the wishes and desires of the man in the pew. Such *a priori* assumptions are subject to review in light of the Roper study.

In the midst of such flattering evidence of "grassroot" support for the denominational leadership, it seems almost improper, and certainly unkind, to ask whether or not these respondents knew what they were talking about. Yet, if the Roper figures are to be regarded as meaningful, we should know to what degree these American Baptist church members were aware of the activities of their national leaders and to what extent they were familiar with the national program.

On this issue the Roper findings show that the constituency was not well informed about the activities of the American Baptist Convention. Only 40 percent even knew that the national offices were located at Valley Forge. Only an additional 2 percent of the respondents gave the less specific but correct answer of Pennsylvania. Also 9 percent of the sample gave incorrect answers, and 51 percent said they "didn't know." The Roper Associates said, "We would guess that correct knowledge of where the national offices are located is even lower in fact than this survey shows, since all respondents were mailed a letter on American Baptist Convention letterhead plainly showing 'Valley Forge'" (Roper, pages 68 and 69).

	Percentage who named Valley Forge %
Total church members	40
Sex	
Men	45
Women	37
Age	
18–34	31

35-54	46
55 and over	37
Race	
White	44
Non-white	10
Educational level	
College	57
High school	36
Grade school	19
Geographic area	
Northeast	41
Midwest	44
South	26
Far West	38
Frequency of worship service attendance:	
Once a week or more	49
Once or twice a month	28
Less often or never	18

The lack of knowledge about the activities of the denomination is openly admitted by most of the respondents. When asked about how much they had heard of the work being done at the national offices or the activities of the Convention's leaders, the large majority (74%) answered, "Not very much," or less than that. Half of those in the sample said that they had heard "very little" or "nothing" about such things. Only 5 percent said they knew "a great deal" about the workings of the denomination and 20 percent claimed to have a "fair amount" of knowledge (Roper, page 70).

Number of respondents	997
	%
How much is heard about leaders and work at national office:	
Great deal	5
Fair amount	20
Not very much	24
Very little	35
Nothing	15
Don't know	1

These figures demonstrate a serious problem in communica-

ᏏᎷ 7 ᏏᎷ 3ᐟ
tion between the national executives and the members in local
churches. The Roper Associates stated: "It is even more scri-
ous in that there is little change in the percentages giving
these answers through the various subgroups of church members" (Roper, page 70).

The blame for this breakdown in communications should
not be placed entirely upon the people at Valley Forge. Indeed, I may have even been too harsh on those in charge of
missionary promotion. The facts are that *the local pastors are
probably the most responsible* for this state of affairs. It is
common knowledge that the local congregations for the most
part have their views and knowledge of denominational activities almost completely determined by their ministers. When
asked to name sources from which they sometimes got news
about the Convention, most respondents cited their pastors or
the media which pastors control. When asked where they got
most of their news about Convention activities, the denomination's newspapers and magazines emerged as the leading
sources of information (Roper, page 17).

	Sometimes get news from	*Get most of news from*
Number of respondents	997	997
	%	%
Local minister	67	29
Church bulletin	63	20
Newspapers or magazines put out by American Baptist Convention	56	34
Pamphlets put out by American Baptist Convention	47	13
Local newspapers	26	3
Television	14	2
Radio	13	2
General magazines	11	2
Other (volunteered)	3	1
None (volunteered)	1	1
Don't know, no answer	2	6

These figures show that the pastors of local churches to a
large degree control the flow of information about the Convention which reaches the denomination's constituency. The

church bulletin is usually compiled by the pastor, so that only those things he approves ever get printed in it. Thus the church bulletin should not be considered as a source of information that is different, or separate, from the pastor.

While the newspapers and magazines put out by the American Baptist Convention represent a significant source of information concerning denominational activities, there is much to indicate that pastors exercise a significant influence over whether these publications ever get into the hands of the constituency. The majority of those who read *Crusader* (formerly the denomination's newspaper) received their copies through the mail (Roper, page 26).

	Total	Readership of Crusader Read monthly	Read less regularly
Number of respondents	632	408	212
	%	%	%
Copies come in mail	78	93	52
Get copies at church	11	6	21
Copies are passed along by friend or relative	8	1	23
Don't know, no answer	4	*	3

*Less than 0.5 percent

The Roper study did not indicate what proportion of these respondents had personally subscribed to this periodical. A careful exploration of this question might have demonstrated that the majority had *Crusader* sent to them because their churches had paid for it. Many churches subscribed to *Crusader* for each family in their respective congregations. If the churches did not assume this responsibility, it is doubtful whether many of these members would have subscribed on their own. Some evidence for this opinion can be found in the reasons for discontinuance by those who had given up regularly reading *Crusader* (Roper, page 25).

Major Reasons for No Longer Reading Crusader Regularly:

Number of respondents	47
	%
Stopped sending it to us, church doesn't give it out	47

Too old, eyesight bad, invalid   13
Stopped attending Baptist Church   9

The most frequently cited explanation given for no longer reading this publication was that it was no longer sent to them and the church no longer gave it out. Further research probably would have shown that it was the pastor who was responsible for influencing the decision to curtail *Crusader's* circulation.

The Roper study failed to explore the influence of the minister with respect to his control of what information about the American Baptist Convention gets to the denomination's constituency. Those who are deeply involved with the activities of Baptist churches know what a serious mistake this is. There is very little question in the minds of denominational executives that the loyalty which a church and its members have for the Convention will be largely determined by the ministerial leadership. A pastor can bring his congregation into a close relationship with the American Baptist program or he can (as has often been the case) be responsible for his church severing its official ties with the denomination. Many a church has been lost to the Convention because a pastor "led his church out."

The people tend to trust their pastor and view the denomination in accord with his opinions. Many pastors will let only that information about the Convention which is supportive of their own opinions pass on to their members. If a pastor is favorable to the denomination, he will pass on those views of denominational activities which he knows will be positively accepted by the congregation. On the other hand, if he is ill disposed toward the American Baptist Convention, he might pass on reports which he knows will agitate his people. He might deliberately ignore those aspects of the denominational program which would gain support from his church members. These statements may be harsh, but in all probability the pastors themselves would openly admit to their validity.

Baptist polity states that the minister is just another member of the congregation, but those acquainted with the latent structure of Baptist churches know this claim to be simply rhetoric. He exercises tremendous control over his people, particularly because he is not subject to any ruling body beyond his own congregation. No denominational executive can tell a local pastor what to do — and the local pastors know this fact and take pride in it.

The significance of the pastor has tremendous importance for denominational program planning. A program which is developed to meet the expressed desires of the constituency is not enough, for if the pastor is not in favor of the program, it may never get to them. There seems to be no way of getting around the pastor, although some state executives have tried. Therefore, a study on the clergy of the American Baptist Convention should be made to find out what they think about the denomination and its program. If they are not enthusiastic about what comes from Valley Forge, it is doubtful that the denominational programs will make much headway. While pastors represent a very small minority of the denomination's membership, their significance is sufficient for disproportionate attention by program planners.

This evidence seems to suggest that the local pastors pass on very little information about denominational activities to their congregations. Therefore, church members know very little about what is going on, but they do have a positive impression of the American Baptist program. Thus, what pastors do pass on is seemingly favorable. The pastors may be keeping news from their people because they think that some of the information might cause various members to become discontented with affiliation with the Convention. Since American Baptist churches have shown a great propensity to schisms and withdrawals by fundamentalist members, a pastor might regard ignorance of denominational affairs as one way to keep the local members from becoming upset. One wonders how the members on the local level might regard the American Baptist Convention if they were aware of some of the views held by prominent leaders on such subjects as the Vietnam War and the Women's Liberation Movement. One sociologist has remarked that American Baptists are Republicans at prayer. However, this picture probably does not fit the *leadership*, and it might be best if the news did not get out.

6

Some Consequences of the Roper Study

A PRIMARY REASON FOR ASKING the Roper Associates to engage
in their study of the American Baptist Convention was to
provide data for a more comprehensive examination of communications from the national offices of the denomination.
Therefore, it is not surprising that the first major policy change
resulting from the study pertained to the publication of *Mission* magazine and *Crusader*.

Changes in Denominational Publications

The results of the Roper research indicated that the Division of Communications was probably wasting time, effort,
and money by putting out two publications, since those who
received *Mission* magazine were, for the most part, also re-
cipients of *Crusader*. Almost three-quarters (72%) of those
who claimed to have read *Mission* magazine monthly also
claimed to have read *Crusader* monthly. An additional 14
percent of the monthly readers of *Mission* said that they sometimes had read *Crusader* (Roper, pages 24 and 25). Such
an overlap indicated that these publications were reaching the

same audience and that *Mission* magazine subscribers were simply a subgroup of the *Crusader* readers. The obvious decision suggested by these findings was to combine the two publications and thus, more effectively and economically, to reach the most members of the denomination with the most news. This move was made in April, 1970, when a new publication, *The American Baptist*, came into existence as a successor to both *Crusader* and *Mission* magazine.

A major change in the policy of the American Baptist Convention is seldom accepted peacefully. The fears and suspicions generated during the Fundamentalist Controversy of the nineteen thirties continue to haunt the denomination and reappear in ugly fashion whenever the executives of the Convention try to bring about an alteration in programming. The creation of *The American Baptist* as a successor to the two earlier publications, *Mission* and *Crusader*, was no exception to this tendency.

Unfortunately, some problems arose over what would happen to the editors of the former publications and who would assume control over the new newspaper. Many people were disturbed when Paul C. Allen, who served effectively for many years as the editor of *Crusader*, resigned his position. Many in the denomination claimed that this action was the result of an attempt by the "liberals" to silence the conservative voice of *Crusader* and to extend the influence of what some considered to be "left-of-center" views which seemingly were apparent in *Mission* magazine, edited by Norman R. DePuy.

Rumors and accusations flowed in whispers, and caucuses of "concerned Baptists" gathered to discuss what could be done about the emerging threat to the theological and political views which they believed to represent American Baptist thinking most fully. Letters were written and objections voiced, but the course of action taken by the denomination's officials was not altered. Allen eventually took a journalistic position with a city newspaper in Harrisburg, Pennsylvania. Norman DePuy has since been appointed the editor of the new paper, *The American Baptist*.

There is little question that Paul Allen was one of the

most influential voices for conservatism within the denomination. His outspoken support for traditional evangelism along with his comparatively conservative views on the civil rights movement and the war in Vietnam earned Allen the backing of a significant segment of the American Baptist constituency. These backers did not remain silent when one of their most articulate representatives moved out of denominational officialdom.

As far as I could ascertain, Allen's departure from office was the result of circumstances *not directly* related to the question of who would be editor of *The American Baptist*. His leaving, however, created more tensions in an already troubled denomination and increased the cynicism among the conservatives of the constituency who seem to have growing feelings of alienation from American Baptist power structures.

Norman De Puy had often departed from "safe" traditional postures as he endeavored to deal with contemporary socio-religious issues in *Mission* magazine. However, those who would label him a liberal will find that he deviates from liberal expectations on many occasions. De Puy can hardly be labeled a conservative either, for his views on Vietnam, abortion, and civil rights stray from any predictable conservative syndrome. The truth is that De Puy is difficult to put in any theological or political category and he terribly upsets those who want people to be neatly labeled like insects in a collection. A controversial personality hardly stills the anxieties of those who fear that conservatives have been out-maneuvered in a struggle for power.

The Roper study provides some interesting information related to the above controversy. The research findings indicate that American Baptists who read both publications recognized little difference between *Crusader* and *Mission* magazine. Almost half (47%) who read both said that the two publications had a similar point of view. About one-quarter (22%) stated that they did not know whether the two publications had similar or different points of view. Only one-quarter (24%) said that the publications represented differing points of view, and most of them claimed that the differences were good. In fact only 2 percent of the sample claimed that the divergent perspectives represented by the two publications was a "bad thing" (Roper, page 35). These statistics suggest that the constituency did not view one publication as distinctly conservative and the other as distinctly liberal.

While there has been some criticism of the new periodical, *The American Baptist*, very little suggests that the constituency is upset because some particular theological and political perspective has lost an opportunity for expression. Thus, while Allen and De Puy may have held differing positions, they both apparently published material that was so representative of the mainstream of American Baptist thought that few were able to recognize points of conflict between them. The constituency hardly would recognize the retaining of De Puy and the leaving of Allen to be a triumph for liberalism if they saw little difference between the respective publications which these men edited.

Another change which has affected the publication patterns of the American Baptist Convention has been the format for *The Secret Place*, the denomination's guide for personal religious devotions. Bruce Mills, longtime editor of *The Secret Place*, retired, and the new editors who took his place executed some significant alterations on the shape, style, and manner of presentation of the material in this booklet. Economic factors played an important role in the change of format. Unfortunately, these changes were introduced just before the publication of the Roper findings. Perhaps if the editors had waited until the Roper statistics were available, they would have been reluctant to alter *The Secret Place* in any manner, for there was substantial support for the publication's old format.

Of the 34 percent of the sample who claimed to use *The Secret Place*, the overwhelming majority (92%) said they liked this publication as it was and only 4 percent said they would like to see it changed. The expressed attitudes toward *The Secret Place* were highly favorable. It was considered as "interesting," "inspiring," "honest," and "simple" (Roper, page 39).

Number of respondents	321
	%
Interesting	81
Inspiring	81
Honest	69
Simple	51
Happy	36
Relevant	27
Grown-up	19
Childlike	5
Complex	2
Irrelevant	2
Sad	2
Dull	1
Depressing	1
False	–
Don't know	3

Such results provide very little justification for the alterations which were introduced to the format of this devotional booklet. The new editors may have somewhat damaged the very good image of the publication by the changes. Interestingly, however, though the new format drew many letters of protest, circulation was not significantly affected.

There were other findings in the Roper study, including such things as statistics on the denomination, the manner in which speakers whom the national offices utilize for promotional purposes are received, and the degree of influence exerted by the denomination's radio program, *The Laymen's Hour*. However, for those who are interested in what the Roper Associates discovered by their research on these subjects, the Appendix to this book will provide summary material.

Some Concluding Remarks

The study made by the Roper Research Associates represents a commendable effort on the part of denominational executives to understand the mind and disposition of the members in local churches. While the Roper methodology had some failings, on the whole it yielded some significant statistics about American Baptists, demonstrated grounds for some of the program plans of national leaders, caused a re-evaluation of time-honored practices, and dispelled some erroneous assumptions about the nature of the constituency.

If there is any criticism which might be leveled at what was attempted, it is that the project did not go far enough. Studies of the disposition of the constituency on the pressing social and religious issues of the day could provide a basis for the resolutions which the denomination makes on such subjects at each of its annual meetings. Instead of asking the delegates to the annual Convention gatherings to vote on positions and issues suggested and formulated by a committee, the constituency might be polled in advance of the annual meeting in order to discover their views of what they deem to be particularly relevant to contemporary situations. In this way the Committee on Resolutions could more fully reflect the mind of the denomination's membership. Too often individuals believe that those in power do not even know, much less act upon, the opinions of those in the church pew. They believe that the pronouncements made in the annual resolutions of the Convention do not reflect them. Such a polling process could help eliminate these suspicions.

If the results of studies such as that made by the Roper Associates were utilized in the molding of denominational policy, some of the alienation that the constituency possibly feels with respect to the decision-making processes in the Convention might be alleviated. The Roper study demonstrated that the typical Baptist had a lack of knowledge and concern about his denomination's program and activities. Sociologists are well aware that such dispositions often result from a sense of powerlessness on the part of persons who sense that their leaders are insensitive and unconcerned with their views.[40]

If the constituency thought that its views had a means for expression and that its positions were given serious consideration in the formation of policy, there might be an increase in the interest shown in denominational affairs. A scientific annual polling of the American Baptist Convention on major issues related to the life of the denomination might accomplish such an end.

Also, there is need to explore in greater depth the theological perspectives of the constituency and to ascertain to what degree these perspectives are expressed in denominational policy and programming. The leaders of the American Baptist Convention should know the consensus of the membership on most theological issues and act accordingly. Studies along the lines of that conducted by the Roper Associates would be a step in that direction.

Appendix
The Summary of Research Results
as Stated by the Roper Associates
(Pages 5-13 of the Roper Study)

IN THIS SECTION OF THE REPORT the major findings of the study as we see them are summarized — and not necessarily in order of importance. Some are specific points that came directly out of specific questions. Others are more general impressions gleaned from a review of the results of a number of questions. In the interests of clarity, only brief statements of the major results that support the findings are made here. In the following section, results are discussed in detail and documented more fully.

1. This study shows that one of the most serious problems facing the American Baptist Convention as far as communications are concerned is that of communication with younger church members (in this study "younger people" are the 18-to-34 age group). Considerably fewer of them reported exposure to or readership of most of the communications media investigated in this study than did older people. They tended to be more critical of the Convention than older people, and they were less active generally in their churches

than older people. The problem was further compounded by the fact that apparently there had already been a falling away from the Convention by younger people, and as a result the percentage of young people who make up the Convention is much lower than their comparable percentage in the population.

— Fewer young people said they got most of their news about the Convention from newspapers or magazines put out by the Convention.

— There was less awareness of *Crusader* and *Mission* among young people.

— Both *Crusader* and *Mission* had lower readership among young people — and this is particularly true of *Crusader*.

— Fewer young people got *The Secret Place* than older people.

— More young people said the Convention was "behind the times."

— Attendance at worship services by younger people, although fairly good in the abstract, was less frequent than that of older people. And fewer of them reported they attended other church services or meetings than older people.

— The percentage of Convention members in the 18-to-34 age group was half that in the total population 18 and over, and the percentage of Convention members in the 18-to-24 group was about one-third that in the total population 18 and over.

2. Another problem faced by the Convention, though not so serious as the youth problem, is that the membership is heavily balanced toward women. Nearly two-thirds (63%) of resident adult church members are women. Male church members, however, though fewer in number than women, tended to be more active in their churches. Like young people, they tended to be more critical of the Convention and were less inclined to read *Crusader* and *Mission*.

3. Perhaps one of the most important findings of this study is that the large majority of church members did not appear to be well informed about the national leadership. Part of the reason for this lack has to be laid to communications from

the national office, but there are indications throughout this study that it is probably equally attributable to a lack of interest on the part of church members. And, while we cannot support it with facts and figures, we get the feeling from a detailed reading of the data that a large number of church members relate most to their own local church and do not see themselves as part of a larger national organization — an assumption which may explain the lack of interest in the national leadership.

- Less than half (40%) of those interviewed correctly named Valley Forge as the location of the national office. Actual knowledge among the membership is probably lower than this, since all respondents in this study received a letter on a Convention letterhead showing "Valley Forge."

- The large majority (three-quarters) said they knew "not very much," "very little," or "nothing" about the leaders and work of the national office. *Crusader* and *Mission* readers were not much better informed, with about two-thirds of them saying they knew "not very much" or less about the national office.

- When asked to pick from a list of words and phrases those that described the national leadership to them, over one-quarter answered "don't know." While the descriptions picked were largely favorable, the two leading ones chosen were the more general words "hard working" and "conscientious," while the more specific and discriminating phrases had lower mention.

- One evidence of lack of interest in the national leadership was shown in that the least popular features in *Crusader* are "news on leadership and job changes," "editorials," and "news about work at national headquarters."

4. *Crusader* was the medium that reached more Convention members than any other single form of communications. Almost two-thirds of the church members claimed to read it sometimes, and two-fifths claimed to read it monthly. *Mission* reached substantially fewer members — about one-quarter said they read it sometimes, and 10 percent said they read it monthly. Readers of both publications tended to be older,

female, white, and frequent attenders of worship services. Critical for both publications is the fact that they both had their highest readership among older people (55 years of age and older) and women and that they met with less enthusiasm among the male and younger readers they did have. The problem among young people seems especially important in that it is on this group that the future of the publications — and the continuing vitality of the Convention — depends.

5. There was high overlap in readers of *Crusader* and *Mission*, and particularly in regular readers. Eighty-two percent of those who were reading *Mission* were also reading *Crusader*. This fact means that the two publications were not reaching different groups of readers, but that *Mission* was basically reaching a subgroup of *Crusader* readers. This is not to say that *Mission* served the same function among the people who read it, merely that it was not reaching a different group. However, of those who were reading both publications, only a small proportion (one-quarter) saw any difference in point of view between the two.

6. Both *Crusader* and *Mission* had large groups of long-term regular readers. Over two-thirds of the regular *Crusader* readers, and well over half of the regular *Mission* readers had been reading the publications five years or longer. *Mission* had a much higher percentage of new regular readers than did *Crusader* — 22 percent who had been reading it less than two years, as opposed to 8 percent for *Crusader*.

7. Few readers of *Crusader* and *Mission* were actually critical of the publications. What comes through in this study is more a lack of real enthusiasm for the publications than direct criticism — particularly on the part of readers under the age of 55 and men. For both publications there are clearly a few types of articles that emerge as most and least popular.

— In the case of both publications few readers rated them as uninteresting. However, the majority (over half of all readers) rated them as "fairly interesting" rather than "very interesting." The appeal of both publications to older people and women was again evident in these answers, with these groups having considerably larger percentages rating them "very interesting" than either younger people or men.

— The most popular features of *Crusader* (in the order named) appear to have been "news about Baptist churches and people around the country," "news about home missions," and "news about foreign missions." Least popular are "news on leadership and job changes," "editorials," and "news about work at national headquarters."

— The most popular features of *Mission* were "articles about home missions," "articles about foreign missions," and "articles on public affairs." Least popular was the "leader's forum."

8. *The Secret Place* had a fairly good-sized group of satisfied readers who used it mainly for personal individual reading and who mostly liked it the way it was and would not like to see it changed. Any problems *The Secret Place* has are not with its readers, but with the makeup of its readers. Like *Crusader* and *Mission,* its readers tended to be older, white, and frequent attenders of worship services. However, unlike *Crusader* and *Mission,* it did not have a high female orientation but is reported received equally by men and women.

— One-third of the church members reported they get *The Secret Place* in their homes.

— The large majority — 92 percent — used it mainly for personal individual reading.

— The large majority — 92 percent — liked it "as it is" rather than "would like to see it changed."

— It had a larger percentage of older readers (38% of those 55 and over) than younger readers (26% of those 18 to 34), and a much higher percentage of readers among white church members (38%) than black (5%).

9. Of four other means of communication explored in this study, *The Laymen's Hour* on radio seems to have been the least effective, while motion pictures and filmstrips, pamphlets and speakers from the national office all appear to be fairly effective, and in differing ways.

— *The Laymen's Hour* on radio was reported listened to "sometimes" by less than one-fifth of the church mem-

bers, and had a very small group of regular listeners (2%).
— Pamphlets seem to have been an effective way of communicating with church members *not reached* by some of the other media — particularly *Faith Is the Key*. One-third of all church members had read one or more pamphlets in the past two years, with *Faith Is the Key* the one most read. Significantly, *Faith Is the Key* had higher readership among younger people than older people and also had a higher readership among men than women.
— Motion pictures and filmstrips were seen by one-quarter of church members in the past two years, with about one-fifth saying they had seen filmstrips and one-tenth saying they had seen motion pictures. Motion pictures and filmstrips did as well among young people as among all church members, which appear to make them one of the more effective ways of communicating with the young.
— Speakers from the national office made a good impression on church members who were hearing them. Over one-quarter said they had heard a speaker in the past two years, and most were favorably impressed. And, importantly, speakers were reaching sizable segments of the membership reached less well through the printed media — men, young people, black church members, and non-readers of *Crusader* and *Mission*. This is particularly true of black church members. A larger percentage of black church members said they had heard a speaker than reported exposure to any of the other media asked about in this study.

10. In their general attitudes toward the role of the local church, evangelism, and baptism by immersion versus transfer by letter, more church members evidenced a progressive view than a conservative view.
— The majority (over two-thirds) of church members took the position that the local church should broaden its main efforts to include helping solve the problems of the community and society rather than concentrating its efforts on reaching new members and giving spiritual support to its individual members. This was particularly true of

younger members, with over three-quarters of them taking this position.

— Almost three times as many church members (45%) endorsed the broadest viewpoint of evangelism as endorsed the most limited viewpoint of evangelism (16%).

— While there was still a sizable division of opinion on accepting unimmersed new members by transfer of letter, over half of the church members approved of it. This was particularly true of younger people and the college educated.

11. In expressing attitudes toward the American Baptist Convention, church members — while not taking extreme positions — showed evidence of dissatisfaction that should be of concern to the national leadership. And importantly, the groups that expressed the most dissatisfaction were key groups — men, younger people, the better educated, and black church members.

— Less than half (41%) said the Convention has kept pace with the times, and significantly twice as many (28%) said the church is behind the times as said it is moving too fast (15%). Men, younger people, the better educated, and black church members were all higher than average in thinking the church is behind the times.

— In choosing from a list of statements about their personal satisfaction with the Convention, the majority (73%) indicated they were satisfied. Nevertheless, one-quarter indicated by their choice of statements that they were considerably "bothered" by things about the Convention. Again, the groups who tended to be more "bothered" than others were men, younger people, the better educated, and black church members.

12. Among the issues, interests, and activities of the Convention explored in this study, there was clear evidence that church members placed high priority on Christian education and home missions. And while foreign missions are considered to be an important activity of the Convention, a sizable group felt too much emphasis was being placed on foreign missions, and the large majority felt that in today's world home missions were more important than foreign missions. Involve-

ment in civil rights and race relations seems to have been an area of controversy. While it, too, was considered to be an important activity of the Convention by a sizable group, there was a division of opinion among various segments of the population as to whether it was getting too much or too little emphasis by the Convention. Men, white church members, and *Crusader* readers tended more to think it was getting too *much* emphasis, while younger church members and black church members tended more to think it was getting too *little* emphasis.

13. Finally — and generally — we get the impression from this study that the American Baptist Convention in its practices, policies, and communications is hitting right down the middle of the road for the present membership. For the present membership, the Convention is not too conservative or too liberal. It is not moving too fast or too slowly. However, it is too conservative, too slow, and too backward for the young and the college educated — the "tomorrow" groups which constitute the growth potential.

Some Questions Raised by the Study

It seems that this study has raised several questions for serious consideration by the national leadership of the American Baptist Convention. And while we fully realize that raising questions is easier than answering them, we nevertheless would like to list the questions as we see them.

1. What can be done both to keep young people in the Convention and to make them more effective church members?

2. What can be done in the area of communications to reach young people and men more effectively? Pamphlets, speakers, and films appear to be effective media with these groups.

3. What can be done to counteract the impression that the Convention is "behind the times"?

4. What can be done to build among Convention members a closer identity with the national organization and a greater interest in the work of the leadership?

5. What can be done to acquaint church members better with the national leadership group?

6. Finally, what can be done to reach and interest the young people who are not joining the Convention in their true proportion?

Notes

[1] See W. Lloyd Warner, *Social Class in America* (New York: Harper & Row, Publishers, 1960).

[2] Herbert Schneider, *Religion in 20th Century America* (Cambridge, Mass.: Harvard University Press, 1952), Appendix, p. 228.

[3] Robert Southey, *The Life of Wesley; and The Rise and Progress of Methodism* (London: Longman, Brown, Green, and Longmans, 1846), vol. 2, pp. 369-370.

[4] The concept of the Protestant ethic and its relation to capitalism had its classical expression in Max Weber, *The Protestant Ethic and the Spirit of Capitalism* (New York: Charles Scribner's Sons, 1958).

[5] Robert G. Torbet, *A History of the Baptists* (Revised) (Valley Forge: Judson Press, 1963), pp. 298-305.

[6] Max Weber, *The Theory of Social and Economic Organization*, translated by A. M. Henderson and Talcott Parsons, edited by Talcott Parsons (New York: The Free Press, 1965), pp. 329-341.

[7] Anthony Campolo, Jr., "A Study of the Controversy in the American Baptist Convention over the Function and Structure of the Church" (Philadelphia: Doctoral dissertation at Temple University, 1968).

[8] Torbet, *A History of the Baptists*, pp. 298f.

[9] This middle-class perspective might be classified as a "Christ the Transformer of Culture" point of view. See H. Richard Niebuhr, *Christ and Culture* (New York: Harper & Row, Publishers, 1956), pp. 190-229.

[10] Paul M. Harrison, *Authority and Power in the Free Church Tradition* (Princeton: Princeton University Press, 1959), pp. 11-16.

[11] Conservatives in the Convention have continually endeavored to have the denomination commit itself to a particular doctrinal statement. See Torbet, A History of the Baptists, pp. 424ff.

[12] Edward D. Rapp and James A. Scott, American Baptists Today (New York: American Baptist Home Mission Societies, 1957), p. 32.

[13] H. Richard Niebuhr, The Social Sources of Denominationalism (New York: The World Publishing Company, 1957), pp. 26-105, explains such a transition as the inevitable result of the movement of a religious group from "sect" to "denominational" status.

[14] Fyodor Dostoyevsky, The Brothers Karamazov, translated by Constance Garnett (New York: The Illustrated Modern Library, 1945), p. 303.

[15] J. Milton Yinger, Religion, Society and the Individual (New York: The Macmillan Company, 1965), p. 93.

[16] David Moberg, The Church as a Social Institution (Englewood Cliffs, N. J.: Prentice Hall, Inc., 1962), pp. 396-400.

[17] Ibid.

[18] S. V. Didato and T. M. Kennedy, "Masculinity-Feminity and Personal Values," Psychological Reports, no. 2 (1956), pp. 231-250.

[19] Frederick Davenport, Primitive Traits in Religious Revivals (New York: The Macmillan Company, 1906), pp. 293-294.

[20] J. Milton Yinger, The Scientific Study of Religion (New York: The Macmillan Company, 1970), p. 134.

[21] Henry Steele Commager, The American Mind (New Haven: Yale University Press, 1950), pp. 166-167.

[22] Ruby Jo Reeves Kennedy, "Single or Triple Melting Pot? Intermarriage Trends in New Haven, 1870-1940," The American Journal of Sociology, vol. 47, no. 4 (January, 1944).

[23] Will Herberg, Protestant — Catholic — Jew (Garden City, N. Y.: Doubleday & Company, Inc., 1955), pp. 53-54.

[24] Peter L. Berger, The Noise of Solemn Assemblies (Garden City, N. Y.: Doubleday & Company, Inc., 1961), especially Chapter II, "The Nature of the Religious Establishment."

[25] "The Preaching and the Power," Newsweek, vol. 76, no. 3 (July 20, 1970), pp. 50-55.

[26] Berger, The Noise of Solemn Assemblies, pp. 90-104.

[27] J. Milton Yinger, Sociology Looks at Religion (New York: The Macmillan Company, 1963), p. 71.

[28] Ronald E. Osborn, The Spirit of American Christianity (New York: Harper & Row, Publishers, 1958), pp. 194-195.

[29] "The More One Is Given, the More Is Expected of Him," study by the staff of the American Baptist Extension Corporation, Valley Forge, Pa., 1970. On file at offices of the New Jersey Baptist Convention.

[30] Ibid.

[31] Emile Durkheim, The Elementary Forms of the Religious Life, translated by T. Swain (New York: The Free Press, n.d.).

[32] Paul L. Stagg, *The Converted Church* (Valley Forge: Judson Press, 1967).

[33] Jitsuo Morikawa, *Pastors for a Servant People* (New York: Division of Evangelism, American Baptist Home Mission Societies, 1961).

[34] Peter L. Berger, *The Sacred Canopy* (Garden City, N. Y.: Doubleday & Company, Inc., 1969), pp. 105-126.

[35] Niebuhr, *The Social Sources of Denominationalism*, pp. 90-105.

[36] Berger, *The Sacred Canopy*, p. 123.

[37] See Seymour M. Farber, Piero Mustacchi, and Roger H. L. Wilson, eds., *Man and Civilization: The Family's Search for Survival* (New York: McGraw-Hill Book Company, 1965).

[38] W. Lloyd Warner and Paul Lunt, *The Social Life of a Modern Community* (New Haven: Yale University Press, 1941), p. 329.

[39] J. Milton Yinger, *Religion in the Struggle for Power* (New York: Russell & Russell, Inc., 1961), pp. 155-158.

[40] David Riesman and Nathan Glazer, "Criteria for Political Apathy," *Studies in Leadership*, edited by Alvin W. Gouldner (New York: Harper & Row, Publishers, 1950).